p 45   p50   p 73   o74   ⊃ ?

C000176473

TRIAL ᴅ̵ʏ̵
LAUGHTER

by Ian Hislop and Nick Newman

‖SAMUEL FRENCH‖

samuelfrench.co.uk

Copyright © 2018 by Ian Hislop and Nick Newman
All Rights Reserved

TRIAL BY LAUGHTER is fully protected under the copyright laws of the British Commonwealth, including Canada, the United States of America, and all other countries of the Copyright Union. All rights, including professional and amateur stage productions, recitation, lecturing, public reading, motion picture, radio broadcasting, television and the rights of translation into foreign languages are strictly reserved.

ISBN 978-0-573-11595-0

www.samuelfrench.co.uk

www.samuelfrench.com

FOR AMATEUR PRODUCTION ENQUIRIES

UNITED KINGDOM AND WORLD
EXCLUDING NORTH AMERICA
plays@samuelfrench.co.uk
020 7255 4302/01

Each title is subject to availability from Samuel French,
depending upon country of performance.

CAUTION: Professional and amateur producers are hereby warned that *TRIAL BY LAUGHTER* is subject to a licensing fee. Publication of this play does not imply availability for performance. Both amateurs and professionals considering a production are strongly advised to apply to the appropriate agent before starting rehearsals, advertising, or booking a theatre. A licensing fee must be paid whether the title is presented for charity or gain and whether or not admission is charged.

The professional rights in this play are controlled by Casarotto Ramsay & Associates, Waverley House, 7–12 Noel St, Soho, London W1F 8GQ.

No one shall make any changes in this title for the purpose of production. No part of this book may be reproduced, stored in a retrieval system, or transmitted in any form, by any means, now known or yet to be invented, including mechanical, electronic, photocopying, recording, videotaping, or otherwise, without the prior written permission of the publisher. No one shall upload this title, or part of this title, to any social media websites.

The right of Ian Hislop and Nick Newman to be identified as author of this work has been asserted in accordance with Section 77 of the Copyright, Designs and Patents Act 1988.

THINKING ABOUT PERFORMING A SHOW?

There are thousands of plays and musicals available to perform from Samuel French right now, and applying for a licence is easier and more affordable than you might think

---

From classic plays to brand new musicals, from monologues to epic dramas, there are shows for everyone.

Plays and musicals are protected by copyright law, so if you want to perform them, the first thing you'll need is a licence. This simple process helps support the playwright by ensuring they get paid for their work and means that you'll have the documents you need to stage the show in public.

Not all our shows are available to perform all the time, so it's important to check and apply for a licence before you start rehearsals or commit to doing the show.

LEARN MORE & FIND THOUSANDS OF SHOWS

Browse our full range of plays and musicals, and find out more about how to license a show
www.samuelfrench.co.uk/perform

Talk to the friendly experts in our Licensing team for advice on choosing a show and help with licensing
plays@samuelfrench.co.uk   020 7387 9373

Acting Editions

BORN TO PERFORM

Playscripts designed from the ground up to work the way you do in rehearsal, performance and study

---

Larger, clearer text for easier reading

Wider margins for notes

Performance features such as character and props lists, sound and lighting cues, and more

---

+ CHOOSE A SIZE AND STYLE TO SUIT YOU

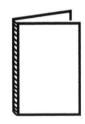

STANDARD EDITION

Our regular paperback book at our regular size

SPIRAL-BOUND EDITION

The same size as the Standard Edition, but with a sturdy, easy-to-fold, easy-to-hold spiral-bound spine

LARGE EDITION

A4 size and spiral bound, with larger text and a blank page for notes opposite every page of text – perfect for technical and directing use

LEARN MORE samuelfrench.co.uk/actingeditions

Other plays by IAN HISLOP and NICK NEWMAN
published and licensed by Samuel French

A Bunch of Amateurs

The Wipers Times

FIND PERFECT PLAYS TO PERFORM AT
www.samuelfrench.co.uk/perform

MUSIC USE NOTE

Licensees are solely responsible for obtaining formal written permission from copyright owners to use copyrighted music in the performance of this play and are strongly cautioned to do so. If no such permission is obtained by the licensee, then the licensee must use only original music that the licensee owns and controls. Licensees are solely responsible and liable for all music clearances and shall indemnify the copyright owners of the play(s) and their licensing agent, Samuel French, against any costs, expenses, losses and liabilities arising from the use of music by licensees. Please contact the appropriate music licensing authority in your territory for the rights to any incidental music.

USE OF COPYRIGHT MUSIC

A licence issued by Samuel French Ltd to perform this play does not include permission to use the incidental music specified in this copy.

Where the place of performance is already licensed by the PERFORMING RIGHT SOCIETY (PRS) a return of the music used must be made to them. If the place of performance is not so licensed then application should be made to the PRS, 2 Pancras Square, London, N1C 4AG.

A separate and additional licence from
PHONOGRAPHIC PERFORMANCE LTD,
1 Upper James Street, London W1F 9DE (www.ppluk.com)
is needed whenever commercial recordings are used.

IMPORTANT BILLING AND CREDIT REQUIREMENTS

If you have obtained performance rights to this title, please refer to your licensing agreement for important billing and credit requirements.

ABOUT THE AUTHORS

IAN HISLOP

Ian Hislop is a writer and broadcaster and has been editor of *Private Eye* since 1986. He has been a columnist for *The Listener* and the *Sunday Telegraph*, and TV critic for *The Spectator*. As a scriptwriter with Nick Newman, his work includes five years on *Spitting Image, Harry Enfield and Chums*, and *My Dad's the Prime Minister*, as well as the films and plays *A Bunch of Amateurs* and *The Wipers Times*. He has written and presented many documentaries for TV and radio including: Radio 4's *The Real Patron Saints, A Brief History of Tax, Are We Being as Offensive as We Might Be, Lord Kitchener's Image, The Six Faces of Henry VIII* and *I've Never Seen Star Wars*. He also presented TV's *Great Railway Journeys – East to West, Scouting for Boys, Not Forgotten, Ian Hislop Goes off the Rails, Ian Hislop's Changing of the Bard, Age of the Do-Gooders, When Bankers Were Good, Stiff Upper Lip: An Emotional History of Britain, Ian Hislop's Olden Days* and *Victorian Benefits: Workers and Shirkers*. In 2018 he co-curated the British Museum's exhibition *I Object: Ian Hislop's Search for Dissent*. He has appeared frequently on *Question Time* and since 1990 has been team captain on BBC's *Have I Got News For You* – which has won many awards including the BAFTA for Best Comedy 2016. Most recently he and Nick Newman wrote the critically acclaimed 2016 Radio 4 comedy drama *Trial by Laughter*. In 2016 their play *The Wipers Times* was premiered and had a successful run at the Watermill Theatre, before a sell-out tour and transfer to the West End.

ABOUT THE AUTHORS

NICK NEWMAN

Nick Newman is an award-winning cartoonist and writer. He has worked for *Private Eye* since 1981 and has been pocket cartoonist for the *Sunday Times* since 1989. His cartoons have appeared in many other publications including the *Guardian, Punch* and the *Spectator*. He was The Cartoon Art Trust's Pocket/Gag Cartoonist of the Year in 1997, 1998, 2005 and 2016. He won the Sports Journalists' Association's Cartoonist of the Year award in 2005, 2007 and 2009. In 2013 he edited the humour bestseller *Private Eye: A Cartoon History*. His scriptwriting career with Ian Hislop began with *Spitting Image*, and continued with Dawn French's *Murder Most Horrid* and *The Harry Enfield Show* – with the creation of Tim Nice-But-Dim. They also wrote the BBC1 film *Gobble* and the sitcom *My Dad's the Prime Minister*. In 2008 their film *A Bunch of Amateurs* starring Burt Reynolds was chosen for the Royal Film Performance, before being adapted for the stage at the Watermill Theatre. In 2014 their film *The Wipers Times* won the Broadcast Press Guild Award for best single drama, and was nominated for a BAFTA, before its stage adaptation and sell-out tour. Radio credits include many series of *Dave Podmore* for Radio 4 with Christopher Douglas and Andrew Nickolds, along with *Mastering the Universe*, starring Dawn French. With Ian Hislop, he also wrote Radio 4's *Gush, Greed All About It, What Went Wrong with the Olympics? The News at Bedtime* and *Trial by Laughter* – dramatised on stage by the Watermill Theatre in 2018, before touring.

AUTHORS' NOTE

Trial by Laughter is a story about the battle for press freedom and free speech. Set in December 1817, it is the true story of the trials of William Hone, a shy, unassuming bookseller and publisher of cartoons and satirical pamphlets. He was taken to court by the Regency government on a charge of seditious libel and blasphemy in an attempt to stifle jokes and criticism of the Tory government and the monarchy. It is both the story of a real life David versus Goliath and a courtroom thriller – with jokes. Or, as we once tried to sell it, *The Madness of King George* meets *Crown Court*.

We are indebted to Janice Hadlow, the former controller of BBC2 for introducing us to the case. Fresh off the back of our BBC2 film *The Wipers Times* Janice enquired if we had heard of a man called William Hone. We both said "Who?" – which is often a good starting point for a story. If a subject is very familiar there may be little new to say. Janice is an expert on Regency history and directed us towards this extraordinary man, who, we discovered, was not only a champion of civil liberties but was also a campaigner for the reform of lunatic asylums and the jury system, an investigative journalist and an ardent supporter of universal suffrage. He lived in poverty with his wife Sarah and (then) eight children (later twelve) and was supported by such literary luminaries as Charles Lamb and William Hazlitt. His partner in crime was the great political cartoonist George Cruikshank, with whom he collaborated on numerous pamphlets and satirical prints.

The persecution of Hone was played out against a rich backdrop of civil unrest, fear of revolution and the wanton licentiousness and corruption of the Regency government. The future George IV was later dubbed the worst king in British history – no mean achievement – and was widely seen as a figure of malevolent fun and ridicule. All these ingredients led us to believe that the trials of William Hone were ripe for dramatization. We began by pitching the idea of a radio play to Radio 4, but with the thought of a stage play firmly in the back of our minds. The courtroom is a natural theatre for drama, and based on the original transcripts of the case, *Trial by Laughter* starring Robert Wilfort and Arthur Bostrom was broadcast in 2016. The reception was favourable enough to encourage us to pitch it as a stage play. We were delighted that the Watermill Theatre in Newbury responded so enthusiastically.

Wherever possible we have tried to maintain historical accuracy – and would plead "artistic licence" in the instances where liberties have been taken. One can only speculate on the nature of the relationship between the Prince Regent and his mistresses – and our characterisation owes much to the political cartoons of the period. We were lucky not only that Hone produced a detailed account of his trials – but also that he wrote a memoir in 1835 which he amended shortly before his death in 1842. What became clear was that although history condemned him to obscurity, he was at the time an immensely popular figure – not just with his literary colleagues such as the caustic critic Hazlitt, who liked few of his contemporaries. "The public befriended me," wrote Hone, whilst trying to explain to that public his motivation behind his highly controversial religious parodies – some of which he later regretted publishing. "For a short time, in my early years, I was a believer in all unbelief," he wrote in 1838. His apologia for his life's mistakes concluded "I have been a lover of the world and its pleasures, a curious observer of men and manners; an insatiable reader in search of truth; an anxious inquirer after happiness." William Hone's liberal humanity shines throughout his autobiography.

The Wipers Times, our previous play for the Watermill was largely about using humour as a coping mechanism. *Trial by Laughter* is more about humour as a weapon, and questions what we should and should not be allowed to make jokes about. Should one be able to make jokes about religion? At what point do those jokes become blasphemy? Where do you draw the line with satire, when poking fun at religion, politics, corruption and immorality? To argue his case Hone sought to reduce the court to tears – not of pity, but of laughter. This was perhaps unique in legal history.

The issues raised by Hone in his trials have not gone away – which is why the story of *Trial by Laughter* is as relevant today as it was in 1817. In an age of gagging orders, celebrity injunctions, D-Notices and fake news, the questions Hone raised about our right to hold authority to account are as pertinent as they were 200 years ago. We will always be in debt to the unsung hero of free speech.

NN

HONE, DRAWN AND COURT

William Hone's battles with the Regency government were inextricably linked to the cartoons of the period – but cartooning as a profession does not come out particularly well from the story. Although Hone and his cartoonist friend and collaborator George Cruikshank worked together to formulate Hone's defence, the cartoons cited in his trials revealed the dependency of cartoonists on patronage – and their willingness, perhaps borne out of desperation, to do their masters' bidding.

In December 1817 the satirist and bookseller William Hone was subjected to three trials on three successive days. He was charged with seditious libel and blasphemy – Hone had dared to attack the Prince Regent and his ally, the Tory government, by parodying the Lord's Prayer and Ten Commandments – among other biblical tracts. In fact, what was on trial was free speech and press freedom – and the cartoonist George Cruikshank was to prove vital to its defence.

Born twelve years after Hone in 1792, Cruikshank was a friend and key collaborator of the older man, who often kept him alive with food and drink. And there was a lot of drink – as Cruikshank said, "I live on gin and water. My mouth lets the gin in, and my boots the water." Together, in the inns and coffee shops around Fleet Street they formulated Hone's defence – based on historical precedent, and citing previous religious parodies in literary and cartoon form. Cruikshank would have been an expert in the latter, coming from a family of cartoonists – his father and brother were noted caricaturists.

However, George was the most celebrated cartoonist of the day, penning scabrous and scatological attacks on the folly and vices of the Prince Regent George, and his ministers. He and his older colleagues Thomas Rowlandson and James Gillray were the equivalent of TV's *Spitting Image* – rude, crude and lavatorial. Many of their cartoons probably wouldn't be published today, so graphic were they. Gillray's image of the Prince Regent as a "voluptuary" suffering "the horrors of digestion" features an overflowing piss-pot in the background – which might make today's editors blanche.

Rowlandson, as well as being a political cartoonist and keen observer of town and country life, was also the author of extremely pornographic cartoons which would make a sailor blush. Cruikshank himself drew the future King's mistress Lady Hertford riding upon him as if he were a coach in a cartoon entitled "Royal Hobby's (sic) or The Hertfordshire Cock Horse".

Cruikshank also collaborated with Hone to depict George as a giant cannon (then called a bomb, pronounced "bum"), with ministers and mistresses queuing up to kiss his "bomb". The accompanying rhyme left little to the imagination:

"...And Castlereagh will low beseech
To kiss a corner of the breech;
And next will come old Georgy Rose
And in the touch-hole shove his nose!"

But as well as highly personal attacks on the prince regent, he also drew attention to the great civil liberty causes of the day, such as the suspension of habeas corpus – or detention without trial – drawing the figure of Liberty herself being hung from a printing press.

Cruikshank and Hone were more than just comic collaborators responsible for what is now seen as a golden age of satire. Hone also sold Cruikshank's prints in his tiny Fleet Street shop, where vast crowds would gather to see the latest attacks on their leaders. They were the standard-bearers for political and judicial reform. It was hardly surprising that Hone's trials became the great *cause célèbre* of the day. A thousand spectators crammed into London's Guildhall to witness Hone defend himself, by making jokes. It was the nut taking on the sledgehammer as Hone faced the combined might of the Crown and government, battling nobbled juries and an overtly biased judge. Cruikshank depicted Hone as the Gamecock of Guildhall, standing up to the turkeys of the law.

Cartoonists might be seen to be standing up to the establishment, but in reality this was not always the case. Much was made in Hone's trial of the fact that Cruikshank's brother brush James Gillray had accepted a pension from the Crown in order to divert his satirical attention from the Prince Regent and the Tory government to Napoleon and the French threat. Essentially he was bought off – and one might justifiably question his moral flexibility.

Cartoonists have always been subject to financial pressures and the consequent demands of their employers. Most cartoonists today have worked for ogres of the press – for the Regency government read the press barons and their political will. Many cartoonists today have been subjected to either knowing or unwitting editorial control. The Danish cartoonists who incurred death threats for drawing images of the Prophet Mohammed did so because they were commissioned to do so – and feared the financial consequences if they did not. I remember one of today's most eminent and caustic cartoonists being forced to "remove the turds" from a political cartoon by his liberal editor. I myself worked for Robert Maxwell's *London Daily News* – and while I never experienced direct censorship, I had no idea whether the cartoons published were subject to a grander Maxwellian plan. And the same is true of the Murdoch press.

So Gillray took the government's shilling to live (and drink) and his great work was compromised as a result. It was lucky for Hone that he did – as it opened up a rich seam of argument in Hone's defence case, as he fought for free speech and the liberty of the press. It should be added that Hone himself was made of sterner stuff – his moral probity was never in doubt – as his numerous bankruptcies and the poverty of his family testified.

The battle for press freedom continues around the world. Recently the Malaysian cartoonist Zunar faced nine charges of sedition – carrying a sentence of forty-three years in jail – for attacking the Malaysian prime minister Najib Razak and his wife. When Razak fell from power earlier in 2018, Zunar said, "I'll miss him."

The torch for free speech lit by William Hone and George Cruikshank still burns brightly.

Nick Newman
September 2018

WRITER IN THE DOCK

Hone's battle in court made legal history. Since I have been the defendant in a few libel trials over the years (well quite a few actually) the producers thought I might be able to give an expert view on libel. Given that I have lost nearly all of these cases I am not sure that I count as an "expert" though I suppose I do know what it is like to pay out large amounts in damages and even larger amounts in lawyers' fees. And there was one case in which a massive figure of £600,000 damages was awarded to the plaintiff, which resulted in a brief period of fame for me in the *Guinness Book of Records*. As I left the court I was so stunned I complained to the waiting reporters, "If that is justice..." and then I couldn't think of anything to say so I concluded "...I am a banana." I was clearly thinking that the justice system was bananas but it came out as nonsense. It will probably be my epitaph.

It did however look as if I had just bankrupt the magazine I was meant to be editing, so the situation was quite serious. I was also once prosecuted for contempt of court, which has a potential custodial sentence, but was cleared by the very wise and brilliant Justice Popplewell. For some reason the Attorney General at the time decided that he was not happy with this obviously sensible verdict and went to the Court of Appeal asking them to overturn the lower court's decision and to consider putting me in jail. I remember standing in the dock looking very nervous as the Appeal Court Judges announced their decision, well aware that this might be my last day of liberty for anything up to two years. I had my toothbrush in my top pocket and was feeling rather nervous. My wife, who was pregnant at the time, was sitting in the court behind trying to look like a suitable object for judicial pity. There were three men in wigs presiding over the case and the senior judge told me that their Lordships had considered the case closely and come to the conclusion that I was, after all, guilty of contempt of court. The fiercest looking man in a wig looked directly at me and added that they were considering the Attorney General's request for a committal. He then took a very long pause, worthy of Simon Cowell at his hammiest on *The X Factor* on television, before eventually saying "...but in this case we have decided on a fine". I was very relieved. To put it mildly.

This is the most threatening it has got for me but it was absolutely nothing compared to what Hone was facing. Two hundred years ago, after publishing satirical versions of the texts that people heard in church, he was charged not just with libel but with the really serious charge of "blasphemous libel". He had already been imprisoned and made bankrupt preparing for the trial and was facing either a long jail sentence or being transported to the colonies – which for many prisoners turned out to be a death sentence. And yet Hone was fearless and managed to conduct his own legal defence and do it brilliantly.

In one of my first trials I listened to the advice of our barrister, who said it would be better if, when I was called by the other side, I did not give evidence. He did not think I would come across well under questioning and thought that my silence would be a safer option. When the time came the prosecuting barrister was delighted and launched into a long speech which began, "In refusing to take the stand Mr Hislop has displayed all the courage of a frozen chicken..." I learned that particular lesson but in subsequent trials when I did take the stand I was frequently told by barristers, "Do not lose your temper and do not under any circumstances try and be funny." I tried to follow the advice but usually ended up getting cross or making jokes and neither was terribly effective.

What is so impressive about Hone is that he spoke for himself for hours, ignored the legal advice and did the opposite, got furious with the injustice meted out to him and was very, very funny indeed. Newton's famous quotation was originally meant to describe the advances in science but it is equally true about journalists and satirists. We stand on the shoulders of giants. Hone's trial was a defining moment for the freedom of the press in this country and if it all seems a long time ago and if it feels as if these battles have largely been won in Britain, I think it is still worth being grateful (and vigilant) about this legacy. It is also worth remembering that the policy of prosecuting your critics for blasphemy, when you really want to stop them criticizing your politics, is still being enthusiastically used by repressive governments all around the world.

Ian Hislop
September 2018

TRIAL BY LAUGHTER

Trial by Laughter was first presented at the Watermill Theatre, Newbury, on 20 September 2018, with the following cast:

LADY HERTFORD . . . . Helena Antoniou
SIDMOUTH . . . . Philippe Edwards
PRINCE REGENT . . . . Jeremy Lloyd
CRUIKSHANK . . . . Peter Lossasso
JUSTICE ABBOTT/DUKE OF YORK . . . . Nicholas Murchie
WILLIAM HONE . . . . .Joseph Prowen
SARAH/LADY CONYNGHAM . . . . Eva Scott
LORD ELLENBOROUGH . . . . Dan Tetsell

Other parts were played by members of the company.

Director	Caroline Leslie
Designer	Dora Schweitzer
Lighting Designer	Matt Leventhall
Sound Designer	Steve Mayo
Musical Director	Tom Attwood
Video Projection Designer	Louise Rhodes-Brown
Movement Director	Emily Holt
Voice Coaching	Elspeth Morrison

Produced by David Parfitt & Bob Benton

A Trademark Touring Ltd & Watermill Theatre Production

This script went to print during rehearsals, and may differ from the text in performance.

CHARACTER NOTES

WILLIAM HONE – thirty-seven. Shy, mild-mannered and genial bookseller and satirist who has the inner steel to take on the Crown and government.

GEORGE CRUIKSHANK – twenty-five (fifty in last scene). The scabrous cartoonist and Hone's partner in crime. Penniless, drunk and dissolute, he renounces booze by the end of the play.

SARAH HONE – thirty-five. Hone's long-suffering but fiercely loyal wife, who is mother to their eight children while running Hone's shop and business when he's in jail.

LORD ELLENBOROUGH – sixty-seven. Hone's nemesis. The bullying Cumbrian Lord Chief Justice who will stop at nothing to win the case.

SIR SAMUEL SHEPHERD – fifty-seven. Crown Prosecutor. Incapable of keeping the trials serious.

LORD SIDMOUTH – sixty. Home Secretary. Keen to pass the buck for the government's failure to stop Hone.

JUSTICE ABBOTT – sixty. Judge in the first trial. Powerless to stop the courtroom descending into farce. Makes the cardinal error of acting constitutionally.

GEORGE, PRINCE REGENT – fifty-four. None too bright and renowned for his debauchery, mistresses and excess, the Prince Regent sided with the Tories to stamp on press freedom.

LADY HERTFORD – fifty-seven. Prince George's mistress, who is a figure of fun in the press and mercilessly (and no doubt unfairly) attacked for her appearance.

LADY CONYNGHAM – thirty-seven. Lady Hertford's love rival in Court. Smarter than Lady Hertford, and considerably more waspish.

DUKE OF YORK – fifty-three. The Prince Regent's brother, who is equally as debauched, and the source of ridicule through the "Grand Old Duke of York" song – which he will never live down.

WILLIAM HAZLITT – thirty-eight. A caustic wit and essayist, Hazlitt despised almost all humanity – but admired Hone.

MR SOUTHALL – thirties. An admirer of Mr Hazlitt.

MARY – thirties. A visitor to Hone while he is in jail, Mary may tempt him, but is not all who she seems.

CLERK IN COURT – twenties. Can't contain his fits of the giggles.

OFFICER – twenties. Initially aggressive, he gets to like and sympathise with Hone.

SHERIFF – twenties. Officious, but unable to control the court.

ELIZA FENNING – twenty. One of Hone's many causes. Hanged for allegedly putting arsenic in dumplings, and victim of a miscarriage of justice – proved by Hone.

MOURNER – thirty. A young writer who admired Hone, but only met him as he was dying.

YOUTH BY BOOKSHOP – seventeen.

CUB REPORTER – twenties.

WEATHERILL – twenty-five. A student who is arrested at Hone's trial.

FOREMAN OF JURY – forties. (may just be a voice off).

FLUNKY – twenties. Cocky and grovelling in equal measure.

TAVERN REVELLER – singer of bawdy songs.

YOUTH

FEMALE ADMIRER/VIEWER

MAN IN CROWD

BALLADEER/TAVERN REVELLER

ACT ONE

Scene One

*Royal Apartments. We hear glorious Handel music.
Outside the Royal Apartment, **LORD ELLENBOROUGH**
and **LORD SIDMOUTH** are rapping at the door.*

LORD ELLENBOROUGH We must see His Majesty!

*A cocky **FLUNKY** appears.*

FLUNKY I am afraid that is not possible.

LORD ELLENBOROUGH What do you mean it's not possible?

FLUNKY His Highness the Prince Regent is indisposed.

LORD SIDMOUTH This is a matter of the utmost importance!

FLUNKY I am afraid I cannot disturb His Highness.

LORD ELLENBOROUGH Why?

FLUNKY He is asleep.

LORD SIDMOUTH It's three o'clock.

FLUNKY Indeed.

LORD SIDMOUTH It's three o'clock *in the afternoon*. Are you
telling me he is still in bed?

FLUNKY Who shall I say called?

LORD ELLENBOROUGH Damn your impudence, you toad eater –
I am the Lord Chief Justice and this is the Home Secretary.
It is imperative that we have his signature on this warrant,
so wake him up or he will be very, very displeased indeed.

FLUNKY I really cannot...

A door opens. **PRINCE REGENT** *appears, wearing a nightgown and hastily putting on a wig.*

PRINCE REGENT What is this commotion? Ah, Lord Ellenborough, Lord Sidmouth I was just busy reading some er...official papers...

We hear the voice of **LADY HERTFORD** *off.*

LADY HERTFORD Georgie-Porgie...come back to bed...

PRINCE REGENT Lady Hertford was assisting me...

LORD ELLENBOROUGH Of course. We wanted you to know that at last we have him!

PRINCE REGENT Who?

LORD SIDMOUTH William Hone, sire. The scurrilous and traitorous publisher of filth.

LORD ELLENBOROUGH He's overreached himself this time.

PRINCE REGENT What has he done now?

LORD SIDMOUTH He has committed a most heinous and blasphemous libel...

PRINCE REGENT Oh God.

Pause.

Has he suggested that I am *fat* again?

LORD ELLENBOROUGH Worse, sire. He has printed a parody of the Book of Common Prayer, which is a grotesque attack on yourself and your ministers and...

PRINCE REGENT I will not have him suggesting I am fat. In one of his publications I was likened to a whale and indeed he called me the Prince of Whales. That's not funny, is it?

LORD SIDMOUTH Indeed not, sire.

PRINCE REGENT Nor clever. And that damned caricature of oneself looking like a blubbery, spouting, sea monster...

LORD ELLENBOROUGH That was Hone's cartoonist accomplice, George Cruikshank, Your Highness.

The door opens again to reveal **LADY HERTFORD** *also in a nightdress.*

LADY HERTFORD Yes, and he turned me into a mermaid. A very fat mermaid.

LORD SIDMOUTH Good afternoon, Lady Hertford.

LADY HERTFORD He always draws me looking fat. I'm not fat, am I, Georgie?

PRINCE REGENT Of course not, my dear. You are no fatter than I.

Embarrassed pause.

LADY HERTFORD It is bad enough that members of society laugh at me behind my back...but to be mocked for the entertainment of the common people is too much...

PRINCE REGENT I'm sure that is not the case, my dear...

LORD SIDMOUTH I'm afraid it *is* the case, Your Highness. You see them massed in Fleet Street around the print shops, guffawing and cackling at the obscene and degrading pictures in the windows! Last week officers had to disperse the mob there were so many! A thousand, they say!

LORD ELLENBOROUGH Which is why it is of the utmost importance that we stamp out this insolence with the full might of the law before this country turns into... France.

LADY HERTFORD *(squeals)* Eeek!

PRINCE REGENT Please refrain from using the "F" word in front of Lady Hertford. I have done my best to remove the offending articles. I have spent a fortune buying up prints.

LORD SIDMOUTH ...which is presumably why they printed more, sire.

PRINCE REGENT *(suddenly touchy)* Are you saying I am, fool?

LORD SIDMOUTH No no, Your Highness.

PRINCE REGENT I am *not* a fool! George Canning told me that he was highly impressed by what he called my "intellectual endowments".

LORD SIDMOUTH My friend Mr. Canning is a very able and wise minister.

There is an awkward pause.

LORD ELLENBOROUGH The point is, sire, that this time Hone has not only traduced Your Majesty's good name, not only has he besmirched the reputation of your ministers but he has also committed an offence against Almighty God.

PRINCE REGENT Excellent! Or rather, how appalling.

LORD ELLENBOROUGH Exactly, sire. This gives us the perfect chance to make an example of this troublemaker and to put out the fires of insurrection that he and his like would willingly fan into naked revolution!

PRINCE REGENT Surely you exaggerate, sir?

LORD SIDMOUTH I believe Marie Antoinette said much the same.

LADY HERTFORD *(squeals, whimpers and faints)* Eeek!

PRINCE REGENT Where do I sign?

LORD ELLENBOROUGH Here, sire, it is an ex officio information...

PRINCE REGENT I don't care what it is, just shut Hone up. I will not be described as a corpulent, licentious, adulterous libertine...

Another door opens. We hear another woman's voice – it is **LADY CONYNGHAM.**

LADY CONYNGHAM Where's my roly-poly Regent?

LORD ELLENBOROUGH Lady Conyngham, good day. I had no idea you were here.

LADY HERTFORD *Neither* had I...

PRINCE REGENT Ah...

Grand, pompous Handel music to denote scene change.

Scene Two

We hear the sounds of Fleet Street in London. Horses and carts, barking dogs, sound of clogs on cobbles. We are outside **WILLIAM HONE**'s *print shop. A* **CROWD** *jostles to look at the prints.* **HONE** *arrives with* **GEORGE CRUIKSHANK**.

HONE Good day to you, sir, good day, madam. What a splendid crowd. Yes, yes, I shall be opening the shop shortly and there are plenty of excellent prints for all to buy and pamphlets starting at a mere tuppence...

CRUIKSHANK ...featuring fine cartoons! By the finest of cartoonists...namely myself.

(to an onlooker) George Cruikshank at your service, madam.

HONE You're too modest, George.

YOUTH Let me see! What's everyone looking at in the window?

HONE That is Mr Cruikshank's latest etching...entitled Liberty Suspended...

CRUIKSHANK And very amusing it is too.

YOUTH Why is the woman being hanged?

CRUIKSHANK It's a joke.

YOUTH Really?

CRUIKSHANK Yes – it's about the suspension of habeas corpus.

YOUTH And what's that?

HONE It is the law that allows the court to determine whether the authorities have the lawful right to detain a prisoner... A right which has recently been viciously and illegally removed...

CRUIKSHANK You see the figure of justice herself being suspended by the very law she has introduced. Clever, eh? And funny.

YOUTH If you say so.

CRUIKSHANK *(tetchy)* You don't like my etching?

YOUTH *(unimpressed)* Not really. I prefer those pictures of Mr Rowlandson...

The rude ones of the ladies with big dugs showing their...

HONE *(interrupting hastily)* Yes, yes... Rowlandson's work is a touch too...graphic for my taste...but we have plenty of other amusing prints...many of them of the amusing Prince...

YOUTH Ha! Good one...

YOUTH *and others laugh.*

HONE A simple pun for which I beg indulgence...

CRUIKSHANK *(annoyed that* HONE *has got a laugh)* My work is for the discerning viewer...like this charming lady here.

FEMALE VIEWER You young wheedle-cutter...

CRUIKSHANK *(to* FEMALE ADMIRER*)* Perhaps I could explain the detail of the drawing over a small glass of something medicinal. *(to* HONE*)* William, I couldn't borrow a few pence, could I?

HONE *fishes out a few coppers for his friend, who exits with* FEMALE ADMIRER. *Another* PASSERBY *doffs his hat to* HONE.

PASSER BY Mr Hone...

HONE Yes, all right, you too...

HONE *puts some change in his hat.* PASSER BY *looks surprised but pockets it.*

HONE *is grasped by an* OFFICER.

OFFICER Are you William Hone?

HONE Yes, and I have no more money today...

OFFICER William Hone, bookseller at 55 Fleet Street?

HONE The same. If you've come from Mr Skeffington, tell him his pamphlets will be ready within the hour.

OFFICER I am an officer of the court and you are my prisoner.

There is a tussle.

HONE Please! Unhand me sir.

CROWD *is unhappy with this arrest.*

MAN IN CROWD What's going on?

OFFICER You keep out of it. Unless you want to be arrested as well.

HONE By whose authority are you acting?

OFFICER I have a warrant from Lord Ellenborough against you.

HONE On what charge?

OFFICER You will find out in due course.

HONE This is unlawful. It is an outrage.

OFFICER I insist that you accompany me, sir, or I shall be forced to place you in grappling irons.

HONE Where are you taking me?

OFFICER You will find that out in due course as well. Come along.

HONE You must at least let me go home and inform my family.

OFFICER I shall do no such thing.

HONE For pity's sake, let me speak to my wife.

OFFICER No, I am instructed to take you directly to the lock-up.

HONE What about bail?

OFFICER Forget about bail. It has been set so high you can't possibly pay it.

HONE I insist that you let me go home.

OFFICER You are not going home for a long, long time...

Scene Three

The Guildhall. We hear CROWD *in the Guildhall in London buzzing in expectation of a trial. We hear a gavel bashing.* JUSTICE ABBOTT *is presiding.* SIR SAMUEL SHEPHERD *is prosecuting for the crown.*

Perhaps a large clockface behind the courtroom action depicts the progress of time, or in reverse, flashbacks.

CLERK The case of the King against William Hone, bookseller and publisher, commencing this day of the seventeenth of December in the Year of our Lord eighteen hundred and seventeen.

Mr Hone is charged with publishing an impious, blasphemous and profane libel with intent to excite impiety and irreligion in the minds of His Majesty's subjects – by ridiculing and scandalising the Christian religion and thus bringing the catechism into contempt. Mr Justice Abbott presiding and Sir Samuel Shepherd, the Attorney General, prosecuting. How does the defendant plead?

HONE *(weakly)* Not guilty.

JUSTICE ABBOTT You will have to speak up, Mr Hone. You are facing a penalty of lifelong deportation to His Majesty's penal colony in Australia or many years' imprisonment at the very least! So I ask you again, how do you plead?

HONE *(stronger)* Not guilty, my Lord. I am unafraid of the penalty, since I am confident the jury will find me innocent.

JUSTICE ABBOTT We shall see. Sir Samuel, if you would like to proceed?

SIR SHEPHERD Gentlemen of the jury, I shall not occupy you long in showing that the effect of Mr Hone's libel upon the catechism, the Lord's Prayer and the Ten Commandments is to denigrate the Christian religion. It is impossible to read it without reaching such a conclusion. And if the Book of Common Prayer is not to be held sacred from ridicule, what is there that is left safe in the mind of a Christian?

SIR SHEPHERD waves HONE's pamphlets at the jury. We hear anti-HONE reaction from CROWD.

If any of you gentlemen be fathers I would ask you this. Would you put these profane works in the hands of your children?

Mutterings of "No".

These works were calculated to weaken the reverence for the Christian faith. It may be said that the defendant's object was *not* to produce this effect. I believe that he meant it, in one sense, as a political squib.

HONE leaps to his feet to interject.

HONE Indeed, that is exactly right, and my point is that...

JUSTICE ABBOTT Pray do not interrupt the Attorney General. Your counsel will have the opportunity to present your defence later.

HONE But I have no counsel.

We hear surprise in court.

SIR SHEPHERD You have chosen to dispense with legal representation? Are you now a legal expert as well as an expert blasphemer?

CROWD *laughs with* SIR SHEPHERD.

HONE *(appealing to JUSTICE ABBOTT)* Members of the jury, I am unassisted by counsel not out of choice but out of poverty – as you can see from my shabby appearance I am as destitute as any man in London. These past months I have been prevented from pursuing my business due to my illegal imprisonment, which has reduced me to absolute penury.

This predicament has been forced upon me and my unfortunate wife and innocent children by the machinations of the Attorney General...

SIR SHEPHERD Machinations? Really?

HONE ...the judicial system, and the entire government.

JUSTICE ABBOTT Mr Hone even if you are representing yourself, you are obliged to obey the rules and procedures of the law. You must at this point remain silent and refrain from making such unfounded allegations – not least against myself.

CROWD *laughs with* **ABBOTT**.

HONE I thank Your Lordship for your advice. I was merely agreeing with Sir Samuel that my intent was always political.

SIR SHEPHERD But it is not the *intent* which is important but the *effect*. And Mr Hone's scandalous parody of the catechism – that sacred summary of the doctrines of the Church of England which are taught to infants so that they might declare their faith – that parody has the unarguable *effect* of bringing the Church into contempt.

Again **HONE** *leaps to his feet.*

HONE Not so!

JUSTICE ABBOTT Mr Hone! Your unfamiliarity with the court's procedure is proving tiresome. What is your objection at this point?

HONE *stands. Shuffles papers, drops them, regathers. He starts weakly but grows in confidence.*

HONE Gentlemen of the jury, I am not in the habit of addressing an assembly such as this. Indeed I have never addressed any assembly before so I beg your indulgence. I stand before you as an impoverished bookseller in poor health and threadbare coat, a humble man ill-equipped to face this persecution by the great powers in the land, from whom I have received nothing but abuse and bad treatment since my summary and unconstitutional arrest in May of this year...

Scene Four

Flashback. We are going back in time to before the trial.

A prison cell, the atmosphere damp and echoey. HONE *is shouting off.*

HONE Release me – I am illegally detained – and I am not a well man.

OFFICER *enters.*

OFFICER Save your breath to cool your porridge! You have a visitor.

Enter SARAH, HONE's *wife, carrying a basket with bread and other provisions.*

Wait there! I'll have to search your basket for any concealed weapons.

He checks the basket, and nicks a pie.

SARAH That's outrageous! That's theft.

OFFICER What are you going to do about it – put me in jail?

He laughs and eats the pie.

You're clear. Ten minutes.

OFFICER *leaves.*

HONE My darling Sarah...

But instead of a fond reunion, SARAH *starts hitting him with a loaf of bread.*

SARAH You idiot! You irresponsible, reckless idiot! Why must you continue to test the patience of the law...

HONE But I'm entirely innocent...

SARAH What you are is entirely stupid! Isn't it enough that your children have no beds and sleep on boards? What is to become of us? There has been a high price to pay for your stubbornness and we, your family, have paid it!

HONE I know, I know...

SARAH And what am *I* meant to do while you languish in jail, a martyr to your noble causes? Feed eight children, run your shop and *then* somehow find the means of getting you out of prison?

SARAH *breaks down.* HONE *consoles her.*

HONE I know I have let you down, I have been a selfish husband and more wedded to my politics than your domestic happiness.

(pause) You do not contradict me?

SARAH I certainly do not! I am a loyal wife and I entirely agree with your low opinion of yourself!

A slight thawing in the air.

HONE You are, as always, right. And I fear I have been a poor father to...Emma, John, Rose, Samuel, Alfred...

SARAH Charlotte...

HONE Charlotte...

SARAH Ellen...

HONE Ellen and...

SARAH Fanny.

HONE Fanny of course. I haven't missed any out, have I?

SARAH No, eight is quite sufficient for a penniless man sitting in a prison cell, don't you think?

HONE What have I done to you? You deserve so much more.

SARAH Again, I must agree with you...

HONE I'm sorry. I ask too much of you.

(pause) So...I don't suppose you've managed to find the money to pay the bail?

SARAH No, I haven't! There *is* no money! You spent it all on your prints and your books! What little money we've had you've given away.

HONE You're exaggerating...

SARAH They say that you are the most generous man in London. They say that when a man takes his hat off in the street to greet a friend, William Hone puts money in it!

HONE That only happened once. And I thought I was giving money to the poor.

SARAH We *are* the poor! You're bankrupt!

HONE I thought perhaps there might still be profits from my pamphlet on the Eliza Fenning case? It did seem to sell very well...

SARAH The money has all gone long ago! And I don't want to hear any more about the Fenning girl. You spend more time worrying about her than you do your own family.

HONE You know that's not true. I worry about you all the time... But it was such a gross miscarriage of justice.

SARAH There you go again. What about the injustice against your family?

HONE Elizabeth Fenning was hanged.

SARAH And so will you be!

HONE Nonsense.

SARAH You don't know what they will do.

HONE I just have to trust that my honesty will be rewarded by good fortune

SARAH You never have any good fortune!

HONE How can you say that? I have you.

There is almost a moment of reconciliation, but **OFFICER** *enters.*

OFFICER Time's up.

HONE I demand to see the legal authorities!

OFFICER And so you will. You can tell it all to the judge. All in the law's good time.

(politely, to **SARAH***)* Very good pie.

Clang as the prison door closes. Another door opens into judge's chambers.

The prisoner William Hone, Lord Ellenborough.

LORD ELLENBOROUGH Mr Hone, before you are tried in court you have to plead to the charges.

HONE But what are the charges? I have been shown no documents and given no explanations.

LORD ELLENBOROUGH You are charged with three counts of publishing criminal and blasphemous libels. How do you plead?

HONE Your Lordship, I am not a well man. Please may I sit.

LORD ELLENBOROUGH *(angrily)* No. You must stand and plead.

HONE Sir, I will not plead until I receive a copy of the charges against me.

LORD ELLENBOROUGH No. It is too expensive to make copies of the charge sheet for every prisoner who is brought before a court. You must plead.

HONE I repeat, please may I sit. I have not been allowed to perform the functions of nature during my incarceration. Please may I sit.

LORD ELLENBOROUGH No!

HONE My Lord, this morning I was found senseless on the floor of my cell and am so weak that I cannot be held accountable for the actions of my bowels and...

LORD ELLENBOROUGH No!!!

HONE *emits a huge fart.*

Really...!

HONE *is removed from the court and thrown back into his cell. Clang of the prison door. Prison cell atmosphere.*

OFFICER A Mr Cruikshank to see you.

CRUIKSHANK *enters, carrying scrolls of paper and a satchel.*

HONE George, it is so good of you to come.

CRUIKSHANK Nonsense! I have been drawing the scene in front of Ellenborough. Is it true that you asked him if you could shit?

HONE No, George. I asked if I could sit...though I did explain about the unreliability of my bowels...

CRUIKSHANK Detail! Detail! You see I have drawn here Lord Ellenborough with a huge fart coming out of his mouth saying, *NOOOO!* ...and there's the clerk with an ear trumpet so he can't hear if you're saying "sit" or "shit". Brilliant, eh?

HONE Have you been drinking?

CRUIKSHANK *NOOOO!* ...but that is only because I find myself temporarily financially embarrassed.

HONE Is that why you came to see me, George? To borrow money?

CRUIKSHANK NOOOOO!!! ...well, yes. Consider it an advance on this print? It's bound to sell well – you can't fail with flatulence – and we can use the profits to pay your bail.

Scene Five

Flash forward to the present. We are back in court.
JUSTICE ABBOTT *bangs his gavel.* **HONE** *is still delivering his defence.*

HONE   ...and not for the first time Mr Cruikshank was being over-optimistic and I remained incarcerated for *months* before finding myself here on trial.

JUSTICE ABBOTT Mr Hone, this account of your imprisonment is not relevant to the case against you. Please allow the prosecution to finish presenting its case.

HONE Indeed I will, Your Honour, but first I thought it only right that the jury should know about the campaign of vilification waged against me by my Lord Sidmouth, the Home Secretary no less, who night after night in the House of Lords has described my works as blasphemy and so has attempted to prejudice my chances of a fair trial.

JUSTICE ABBOTT Mr Hone, I do hate to interrupt your tale of woe but you really must defend yourself against the specific charges brought against you by the Attorney General.

HONE That is my intention...

JUSTICE ABBOTT I am pleased to hear it.

HONE But first I must appraise the jury of the sinister attempt to ensnare me in a treasonable plot whilst I was being illegally incarcerated in the King's Bench Prison...

Scene Six

Flashback. We are back in the cell. We hear the rattle of keys and sound of the cell door opening.

OFFICER Are you decent Hone? You have a visitor.

An educated but impoverished woman, MARY, enters. She is furtive, but brings food.

HONE *(coughing)* Do I know you, madam?

MARY I'm Mary, sir. I come from Mr Oliver.

HONE And he is...?

MARY One who knows you and your work and would consider it a privilege to assist you in some way. I bring you food, sir.

HONE Thank you! Though I think you may need it more than I.

She sits beside him, perhaps too close.

MARY No, sir. But may I express my deep sorrow at finding such a great man in such a sorry state?

HONE I am grateful to you, madam.

MARY Indeed your pitiable condition matches that of the country which labours under the burden of poor harvests, crippling war debts and tyrannous oppression with the people greatly distressed and the whole population of some districts ripe... for anything.

HONE What are you suggesting?

MARY *offers him a bowl of fruit.*

MARY That with proper leadership and encouragement the people can overthrow the government.

HONE I have always been of the opinion that patience and right-thinking will encourage even those suffering most to redress their grievances through constitutional means.

MARY But surely you agree with Mr Oliver that immediate action is required. We need a show of strength in London. You must know like-minded people in Birmingham? Liverpool perhaps? Or Leeds?

HONE Well I...

MARY I would be glad, no, honoured to take letters to any of your friends in any of these places if it would assist in obtaining a complete victory over this government's reign of terror.

HONE You have mistaken your man, madam. You are a stranger to me, as is the mysterious Mr Oliver. I have no secrets and no sentiments to express beyond those I have stated in print which is that I deprecate all attempts to goad or incite the people to acts that would endanger public safety.

MARY It is a shame that such a noble and respected champion of liberty should entertain such scruples.

> **MARY** *takes back the bowl of fruit on offer.* **HONE** *is further incensed.*

HONE What scruples I entertain are derived from my long-held beliefs. My journal, you will note, is called the Reformists' Register. Not the Revolutionarys' Register.

MARY Your lack of zeal is sadly regrettable. These times call for stout hearts not milk livers.

HONE Well I'm sorry to disappoint you. Let me quote you a poem:
"Come Britons Unite, and in one Common Cause
Stand up in defence of King,
Liberty, Laws;
And rejoice that we've got such a good Constitution,
And down with the barbarous French Revolution"

MARY I've heard better.

HONE Do you know who wrote that poem? Myself, aged twelve. Four years after the Revolution.

MARY Surely you've changed your views since you were a schoolboy?

HONE Some of them – but not my unshakeable conviction that blood is not the answer!

MARY But you must feel that the country groans under the yoke of despotism...

HONE What I feel, madam, is that I need to relieve myself... urgently...so if you will excuse me...

HONE *ushers her out of the cell urgently. She exits.*

That is indeed a relief.

Scene Seven

Flash forward to present. We are back in court. Hubbub.

JUSTICE ABBOTT In what way does this unsavoury anecdote pertain to the charges which I must once again implore you to answer?

HONE This "anecdote" illustrates the unsavoury depths to which my enemies will stoop to try and silence me. Members of the jury may be interested to know that the man who sent this woman Mary – the so-called revolutionary Mr Oliver – was later revealed by the Morning Chronicle to be a government agent. And he and his friends were in the employment of none other than the Home Secretary Lord Sidmouth and the Prime Minister Lord Liverpool...

Surprise from **CROWD**.

If they had succeeded in their entrapment the charge I would now be facing in this court would be treason. And the penalty would be...death!

HONE *sits down triumphantly.*

(to **CRUIKSHANK***)* I think that went well...

CRUIKSHANK For the prosecution, perhaps.

HONE What? I'm making good points.

CRUIKSHANK You're coming across as a self-pitying whinger. You're on the back foot. Where are the jokes?

HONE This is a court of law, George, not a theatre!

CRUIKSHANK Then make it one! You're playing the court's game. Play your game instead. Make them laugh...that's what we do. Laugh them all to scorn!

HONE Really?

CRUIKSHANK Make the jury see the absurdity of the case against you by turning your oppressors into laughing stocks. You've got to trust me!

HONE Oh dear.

HONE has, however, realised that CRUIKSHANK is right.

JUSTICE ABBOTT Mr Hone, the Attorney General is now going to continue with the case against you, and I will have no more of your stories of alleged mistreatment which does not pertain to the sting of the blasphemous libel. Given the irregularities of your presentation, I must ask you again, whether you wish to appoint counsel.

HONE I will have no counsel.

JUSTICE ABBOTT Is that wise?

HONE It's certainly cheap.

We hear titters in CROWD, his first laugh in court. HONE enjoys the moment, and is emboldened.

SIR SHEPHERD Contrary to what Mr Hone claims, the jury will see that his offence is not political but sacrilegious. Take the Apostles' Creed. We all say, "I believe in God, the Father Almighty, creator of Heaven and Earth, I believe in Christ, his only son, our Lord" and so on. Perhaps Mr Hone would like to tell us what was in his disgraceful version? Or is he too ashamed?

(pause) I can't hear you, Mr Hone.

HONE rises.

HONE My version reads as follows... "I believe in George, the Regent Almighty, maker of New Streets and Knights of the Bath..."

We hear titters in court. SIR SHEPHERD looks around angrily. HONE starts to ham it up, lampooning a man of the cloth.

"...and I believe in the present ministry, his only choice, who were conceived of Toryism, brought forth of William Pitt, suffered loss of place under Charles James Fox, were execrated dead and buried..."

Titters turn to laughter.

(raising his voice above the noise) "In a few months they rose again from their minority, they reascended the Treasury benches and sit at the right hand of a little man in a large wig."

Laughter turns to guffaws. **CRUIKSHANK** *gives* **HONE** *a thumbs up.* **JUSTICE ABBOTT** *bashes the gavel.*

JUSTICE ABBOTT This is not a matter for laughter!

More laughter. More gavel banging.

If anyone considers that this case is a subject of merriment then they will soon learn otherwise. They will not be allowed to interrupt those of us gravely performing our duty.

SIR SHEPHERD My Lord, I do not believe that any Christian gentleman of the jury will find any humour whatsoever in the defendant's sacrilegious parody of the Ten Commandments.

HONE Shall we see? Perhaps I could read them out?

Laughs from **CROWD**.

JUSTICE ABBOTT No, perhaps the *Clerk* could read out the offending article, Sir Samuel, his solemn tones may settle the prevalent outbreak of levity.

SIR SHEPHERD I am indebted to you, My Lord. Clerk – read out the offending material to the court.

CLERK "The Minister's Ten Commandments. Thou shalt have no other patron but me. Thou shalt not support any measures but mine. Thou shalt not take the pension of the Lord thy Minister in vain."

Titters break out again.

(beginning to get the giggles himself) "Thou shalt not call starving to death murder. Thou shalt not call royal gallivanting adultery. Thou shalt not say that to rob the public is to steal. Thou *shalt* bear false witness against the people..."

CLERK *can no longer control himself with laughter. We hear laughter and cheers in court.*

JUSTICE ABBOTT I think the jury has heard enough of the heinous libel...

HONE *Alleged* libel, Your Lordship.

SIR SHEPHERD How can *THIS* be alleged, Your Lordship? The libel is self-evident and there is worse. Mr Hone parodies the Lord's Prayer itself.

We hear gasps from one or two in the audience.

Yes – the most solemn prayer to the Almighty, to the Redeemer of the world and to the Holy Ghost, the most sublime part of the public service of the Church. And he does so thus, *(reads)* "Our Lord who art in the Treasury, whatsoever be thy name, thy power be prolonged, thy will be done, throughout the empire, as it is at home..."

Laughter building.

HONE You read it beautifully, Sir Samuel.

SIR SHEPHERD *(speeding up in his embarrassment)* "...give us this day our daily sops, and forgive us our occasional absences from Parliament as we forgive not them that vote against thee, turn us not out of seats but keep us in the House of Commons, the land of pension and plenty, and deliver us from the people, Amen."

We hear a huge cheer and applause from **CROWD**. *More gavel banging.*

JUSTICE ABBOTT I will not tolerate this disruption!

SIR SHEPHERD Thank you, My Lord, but I for one am grateful for this outburst of facetiousness. For is it not a perfect demonstration of the prosecution's case that Mr. Hone's pernicious and profane publication has an immediate and baneful effect upon the public?

Boos from **CROWD.**

And is it not therefore conclusive proof that the lower-classes of society are not fit to cope with the sort of topics that are raised by it?

More boos from lower-class **CROWD,** *who have been insulted.*

I rest my case...

JUSTICE ABBOTT *(disappointed)* Really? Then would Mr Hone like to present his defence to the charge of blasphemous libel?

HONE My Lord, you say it is a libel but it is not a libel until the Gentlemen of the jury say it is a libel.

Laughter in court.

And I say it is a parody and parody is an art that is as old at least as the invention of printing itself. Moreover, I have never heard of a prosecution for parody either religious or any other. You see before me on this table my books and it is from them that I must draw my defence.

JUSTICE ABBOTT Are they legal books?

HONE Yes, My Lord. Quite legal. None of them has ever been prosecuted.

Laughter.

Yet they all contain parodies and the truth is that throughout the history of literature, writers have parodied religious texts and these have never been construed as blasphemy.

Consider this example written in 1518 – a parody of the First Verse of the First Psalm. *(HONE performs theatrically.)* "Blessed is the man that hath not walked in the way of the Sacramentarians, nor sat in the seat of the Zwinglians, nor followed the counsel of the Zurichers".

Confusion in court.

Perhaps not the most humorous lines ever written but a parody nonetheless. And who, gentlemen of the jury, wrote this? *(pause)* A man who everyone in this court would esteem, a man to whom we are indebted for liberty of conscience and to all the blessings of the Protestant Reformation – that man is Martin Luther.

Gasps.

Would any man here say that Martin Luther was a blasphemer? Sir Samuel? Justice Abbott? Any of these distinguished observers?

Gestures to audience. Laughs from CROWD.

And yet he was a parodist just like myself.

JUSTICE ABBOTT The law does not allow one offence to be vindicated by another. I think it best that the defendant shall not read out such things.

HONE I'm sure you do. But I must go on with these parodies or I cannot go on with my defence.

You call my parody of the Lord's Prayer sacrilegious. Yet I have in my hand a parody of the Lord's Prayer delivered in the pulpit by Dr John Boys, the Dean of Canterbury Cathedral, in 1613. *(HONE performs theatrically again.)* "Our Pope which art in Rome, Hellish be thy name..."

CROWD *laugh, they have got this joke.*

JUSTICE ABBOTT You cannot be allowed to proceed in reading a profane parody on the Lord's Prayer. You may only state in general terms that there is such a parody existing.

CRUIKSHANK *(coughing into hand, but audibly saying…)* Claptrap!

This is taken up by the **CROWD**, *who copy him coughing, "claptrap".*

JUSTICE ABBOTT Order in court! I repeat to Mr Hone that to present previous parodies is the same thing as a person charged with obscenity presenting other obscene volumes in his defence.

CRUIKSHANK Good idea! Go on then!

HONE *(tongue in cheek)* Obscene, My Lord? That is an appalling slur on the reputations of devout men of God. These are not obscene volumes but works by some of the most eminent churchmen in the country. Take this by the distinguished author the Reverend Mark Noble, who writes comically about a non-believer who says that: (**HONE** *performs again.*)

"All the books of Moses

were nothing but supposes;

that he deserves rebuke, sir,

who wrote the Pentateuch, sir;

that as for Father Adam

with Mrs Eve his madam

and what the serpent spoke, sir,

was nothing but a joke sir."

Laughter.

The good reverend uses biblical stories for humorous effect – as do I. But no one suggested he was a blasphemer – and this upstanding clergyman also provides my defence in a nutshell: "'Tis nothing but a joke, sir."

Laughter.

Scene Eight

Flashback. A tavern. Laughter, clink of glasses, music.

HONE I'm thinking of quoting the sermons of Bishop Latimer...

CRUIKSHANK William, please tell me you are not going to quote Latimer? You'll end up on another charge of boring the jury to death.

A man arrives and sits at the table with them. It is **WILLIAM HAZLITT** – *literary scourge of society.*

HAZLITT Can I also point out that Bishop Latimer was burnt at the stake. Not a happy precedent?

CRUIKSHANK Oh good – Hazlitt is here to cast his usual good humour on proceedings.

HONE Good evening, William. We were discussing how I might conduct my defence.

HAZLITT There is little point. It is a bag of moonshine. You will of course lose. Leigh Hunt lost, William Cobbett lost...

HONE Cobbett's defence was weak. He merely apologised for causing any offence rather than presenting a robust case for the validity of his writings.

HAZLITT And Ellenborough sent him to jail. Where he will surely send you. If you're lucky. Look at the Fenning girl. They were happy to let her swing and she – as you have rightly, if somewhat repetitively, pointed out – was completely innocent. Whereas you are quite clearly guilty of offending the ministers of the Crown!

HONE Thank you for those kind words, old friend.

HAZLITT I'm merely saying that Eliza Fenning was charged with poisoning her employers. You are charged with poisoning the entire country!

HONE I am aware of that.

HAZLITT As a lowly maid, poor Eliza was made an example of, to reassure her betters that it was unwise for servants to contemplate murdering their masters. And in an exact and rather pleasing metaphorical parallel, you, as a lowly hack, must not be allowed to get away with attacking your political masters...

HONE George, come to my rescue.

CRUIKSHANK I'm sure all will go well. *(pause)* But if it doesn't, can I have your hat?

They all laugh.

HAZLITT And I will eat it if you win. The members of the special jury will be selected by the Crown Office and paid a guinea each to make very sure they find you guilty.

CRUIKSHANK Well that's a cheering thought. Is it not time that you bought a drink, Hazlitt?

HAZLITT Do you not think you have drunk enough, Cruikshank?

CRUIKSHANK I live on gin and water. My mouth lets the gin in and my boots the water.

HONE Hazlitt, I shall confound you. I shall challenge the Crown Office, I will demand a fair selection of jurors, and I shall be tried by an honest body of my peers!

Pause.

HAZLITT My apologies. It is not Mr Cruikshank but Mr Hone who has drunk too much. Your faith in your fellow countrymen is touching, if naive.

*A balladeer in the tavern sings a period song **"MEN OF ENGLAND"** by Shelley.*

BALLADEER

MEN OF ENGLAND WHEREFORE PLOUGH
FOR THE LORDS WHO LAY YE LOW?
WHEREFORE WEAVE WITH TOIL AND CARE

THE RICH ROBES YOUR TYRANTS WEAR?

WHEREFORE FEED AND CLOTHE AND SAVE,
FROM THE CRADLE TO THE GRAVE,
THOSE UNGRATEFUL DRONES WHO WOULD
DRAIN YOUR SWEAT – NAY DRINK YOUR BLOOD?

THE... SEED YE SOW, ANOTHER REAPS;
THE... WEALTH YE FIND, ANOTHER KEEPS;
THE... ROBES YE WEAVE, ANOTHER WEARS;
THE... ARMS YE FORGE, ANOTHER BEARS.

WITH PLOUGH AND SPADE AND HOE AND LOOM
TRACE YOUR GRAVE AND BUILD YOUR TOMB
AND WEAVE YOUR WINDING-SHEET – TILL FAIR
ENGLAND BE YOUR SEPULCHRE.

Scene Nine

Flash forward to present. The clock spins forward. Back into court.

JUSTICE ABBOTT Mr Hone, your persistence in quoting obscure and irrelevant texts is beginning to weary the jury.

HONE Really, My Lord? I note that they are not too weary to laugh.

Laugh from **CROWD**.

And I trust the wisdom of the jury entirely, particularly now that the special jury system has been abolished this very year, after my successful petition.

JUSTICE ABBOTT That issue has been resolved and we do not need to be reminded of it.

HONE Indeed, My Lord, there is no need to remind *anyone* of the previous rigging of the special juries in which out of a list of five hundred possible jurors, some two hundred and twenty-six were discovered to be disqualified by non-residence...

We hear intake of breath.

...or actually dead!

Laughter in court.

...and of the remainder, a mere forty names were regularly selected by the Crown Office to follow the direction of the judge, thus turning trials for libel into what has been described as "a melancholy farce".

JUSTICE ABBOTT Would the defendant refrain from reminding the court of what he promised not to remind us?

HONE The bench may rest assured that I will not mention again...the grotesque mockery of justice that rendered the special juries into puppets of the Crown, sending the innocent to their doom.

JUSTICE ABBOTT Are you questioning the propriety of the justice system? To which so-called "innocent" do you refer?

HONE Elizabeth Fenning comes to mind.

JUSTICE ABBOTT Ah yes, the celebrated "dumpling" poisoner. We are all very familiar with your interest in the case, but I see no reason why this squalid act of domestic murder...

HONE No one even died! The family all recovered fully from the alleged killer dumplings. The only person who was murdered was Eliza Fenning – by the state.

JUSTICE ABBOTT The girl was a trollop who attempted to murder her employers because they disapproved of her numerous seductions of male members of staff...

HONE It is fortunate the dead can't sue for libel.

JUSTICE ABBOTT She was rightly convicted after a fair trial.

HONE A travesty of a trial and an honest appeal rejected by Lord Ellenborough, who made sure that she was sent to the gallows.

JUSTICE ABBOTT Your imagination knows no bounds, Mr Hone! Your version of this story would not be out of place in a cheap novel of the type to be found in a travelling library!

A few titters in court.

HONE Mine was a proper investigation which proved beyond doubt that the law of England had been converted into an instrument of vengeance and an engine of oppression.

JUSTICE ABBOTT Now you are defaming the court as well as the government! Is there no limit to your offensiveness?

HONE I will tell you what was offensive – and that was witnessing the execution of that poor girl. When I found myself standing beneath Eliza on the gallows at Newgate all I saw was fear, bewilderment and innocence...

Scene Ten

We are suddenly with HONE *at Newgate. He is staring
up at the figure of* ELIZA FENNING *on the gallows with
a noose around her neck. Drum roll.*

FENNING   I am innocent. But despite my innocence I offer
prayers for my accusers. I trust to a merciful God, who
knows the most secret thoughts of all our hearts, that he
will grant me grace. I wish to leave the world – it is all
vanity and vexation of spirit. But it is a cruel thing to die
innocently. Before God, I die innocent!

FENNING *drops. Gasp from* CROWD. HONE *is appalled.*

Lighting changes and we return to the court.

Scene Eleven

Courtroom atmosphere.

JUSTICE ABBOTT All very affecting, Mr Hone, but what has it do with your case?

HONE Everything! It was an instance of cruelty that exposed a world of corruption. The hanging of an innocent person is something more than a bagatelle. If the people are not moved into some indignation at the neglect of their so-called guardians, the healthy spirit of society is defunct, and the community is degenerating into a base rabble. Similar to that which marked the declining Empire of Rome.

JUSTICE ABBOTT *(increasingly angry)* We do not have the time to chart the long, drawn-out fall of the Roman Empire. And we are certainly not here to retry Miss Fenning for murder.

HONE Oh no, this is much more serious – we are trying *me* for making jokes!

Laughter in court.

Very well. I shall now move on to another very interesting and pertinent example of historical parody...

JUSTICE ABBOTT *(groans)* And what is this one?

HONE It is a very special parody. It is an illustration by the late Mr. Gillray, a most admirable caricaturist.

Murmur of anticipation. We see the offending cartoon held up.

And I call my expert witness, the celebrated cartoonist Mr Cruikshank, to help us fully understand the cartoon.

CRUIKSHANK *comes to the stand.*

Mr Cruikshank, you are, are you not, an expert on political satire in graphic form?

CRUIKSHANK I am indeed.

HONE And how would you rank Mr Gillray?

CRUIKSHANK I think he is considered to be the *second* finest cartoonist of the age. Some of his most famous drawings of the Prince Regent have been considered almost as successful as my own.

JUSTICE ABBOTT What do you mean by "successful"?

CRUIKSHANK I mean that they annoyed him hugely!

Big laugh in court.

JUSTICE ABBOTT You are clearly not an expert – but merely a cheap peddlar of obscene images of His Royal Highness.

CRUIKSHANK I dispute that, My Lord! My tribute to the Prince Regent on his birthday was not just a picture of him enjoying the company of another man's wife...

Laughter.

...but if you look out of the window behind, you will see that he is merrily dancing a jig while the poor are being hung from Tyburn Tree.

HONE It is in other words a political commentary on the Regent and his government...

CRUIKSHANK *(heavily ironic)* Oh yes! Though it is quite an amusing drawing of a plump fellow and his well-endowed lady friend...

HONE *(hastily)* ...thank you Mr Cruikshank...

JUSTICE ABBOTT What *is* your point, Mr Hone?

HONE My point is that politics, not religion, is at the heart of this attempt to suppress satirical expression.

HONE *holds up a large print of Gillray's cartoon.*

Mr Cruikshank, as an expert, when you look at this cartoon of James Gillray, what do you see?

CRUIKSHANK A large fee.

Laughs from CROWD.

HONE *(exasperated)* Yes and what else?

CRUIKSHANK *(examining the cartoon)* The work depicts a biblical scene and references biblical texts in a parody of the Book of Job. Good old Job, where would we cartoonists be without him?

HONE *(sending up the prosecutor's style)* We see here, do we not, the Duke of Bedford, a prominent Whig, drawn as a whale and riding on his back is Whig leader Mr Charles James Fox, accompanied by other Whig notables all wearing red French revolutionary caps.

Laughter at the drawing.

It is a parody that is sympathetic to the Tory government, would you agree?

CRUIKSHANK Of course it is! It represents the opposition as bloodthirsty Jacobins intent on overthrowing British democracy! There's Charles Lamb as a toad. Coleridge as a donkey. Very, very cruel and unfair. I like it.

Laughter.

HONE And what else does your seasoned eye detect?

CRUIKSHANK Well, old Gillray depicts the liberal press as monkeys with their bums hanging out of their britches... and the figure of Justice as an old hag with her withered boobies on display...

Laughter in court.

JUSTICE ABBOTT Really, Mr Hone, is this fitting material for a court of law?

HONE *(triumphantly)* Yes it is, My Lord, because what the jury do not know is that the cartoon is not merely sympathetic to the government but was drawn by a man who until his death received a pension from His Majesty's government itself!

Outrage amidst CROWD.

JUSTICE ABBOTT You must not make these assertions! What evidence do you have to make such claims?

CRUIKSHANK Gillray told me. And very generous it was too.

HONE And that is not all. This biblical parody was not only paid for by the government but was actually *written* by a member of the government. And not just *any* member of the government but a senior member of the Cabinet.

JUSTICE ABBOTT To whom are you referring?

HONE That member of the Cabinet is none other than the Right Honourable George Canning!

Shock, gasps and uproar. CRUIKSHANK *nods enthusiastically.*

...A serving government minister who is now one of my *prosecutors*!

More shock, gasps and uproar.

(shouting above the noise) And has Mr Canning been arrested? Is Mr Canning standing before you accused of blasphemy? Will Mr Canning be going to jail?

CROWD *jeer.*

I think not.

CRUIKSHANK Shame!

CROWD *uproar of booing and joining in with cries of "Shame".*

JUSTICE ABBOTT If these intemperate interruptions are persisted in, I shall order the court to be cleared!

HONE My Lord, the very men who now prosecute me affecting a regard for religion were formerly guilty of the offences of which I have been accused. Their zeal for religion is false! They are enraged against me for my political opinions! It is plain that the object of Mr Canning's parody is the same as my own. It is political. Yet when the Tories create a libel they escape with impunity.

CRUIKSHANK Quite right! Or rather quite wrong!

Boos, jeers, stamping.

JUSTICE ABBOTT I will have order in my court!

HONE If I am to be punished and not Mr Canning, then a great injustice would be done, and the people of England would determine that theirs is not a free government, but an arbitrary despotism!

Cheers of CROWD, *gavel banging, cheers subsiding.*

JUSTICE ABBOTT The jury will now retire to reach its verdict according to their consciences. My job, gentlemen, is of course, to assist and not to direct you. However I am fully convinced that Mr Hone's publication was highly scandalous, irreligious and libellous.

CROWD *boo in disapproval again.* JUSTICE ABBOTT *repairs to chambers leaving* CRUIKSHANK *and* HONE *alone.*

CRUIKSHANK Well done, William! You were magnificent! Six hours without a break.

HONE I feared I had exhausted all my arguments. I've certainly exhausted myself.

CRUIKSHANK Perhaps we should repair to the Southampton Arms while the jury contemplate their decision?

HONE A sound idea, George.

CLERK *(voice off)* The jury has returned!

CRUIKSHANK *(disappointed)* What? That was quick. They have only been out for fifteen minutes! It is a good sign.

HONE You think so?

CRUIKSHANK Or a very, very bad one.

HONE Thank you, George.

Buzz of expectant court.

JUSTICE ABBOTT Foreman of the jury, Mr Bowring. Do you find the defendant William Hone guilty or not guilty?

FOREMAN *(voice off)* Not guilty!

CROWD *erupts.*

CROWD *(chanting)* Long live the honest jury! An honest jury forever!

JUSTICE ABBOTT Clear the court!

CRUIKSHANK Congratulations, William! You've done it! You've won!

HONE I didn't win. It was divine providence.

CRUIKSHANK ...that cleared you of blasphemy?

Gavel bangs.

JUSTICE ABBOTT Mr Hone, you are free to go.

CRUIKSHANK To the Southampton Arms! The drinks are on... *you!*

Scene Twelve

Pompous Handel music. **LORD ELLENBOROUGH** *and* **JUSTICE ABBOTT** *are striding towards the Royal Appartments.*

LORD ELLENBOROUGH *(furious)* No, Mr Justice Abbott, an acquittal is not a satisfactory result.

JUSTICE ABBOTT I am sure that you can explain the problematic nature of the case to His Majesty.

LORD ELLENBOROUGH I'm not explaining it! You can tell His Royal Highness how you singularly failed to deliver the expected conviction.

JUSTICE ABBOTT Technically it was not *I* in the role of judge but Sir Samuel Shepherd as Attorney General who fell short of persuading the jury of the merits of the Crown's case.

LORD ELLENBOROUGH Nonsense! It was your court and *you* can recount to His Majesty yourself how you came by this dismal outcome...

JUSTICE ABBOTT I came by it constitutionally.

LORD ELLENBOROUGH An elementary mistake.

They come to a halt outside the door to the Royal Appartments. **LORD ELLENBOROUGH** *bangs on the door.*

LORD ELLENBOROUGH Where's the damned flunky? Do I have to open the door by myself?

FLUNKY *appears.*

FLUNKY Good evening, sir.

LORD ELLENBOROUGH No, it isn't! And your opinion on it is of no interest! We are expected by His Highness, so get out of the way!

FLUNKY *opens the door to laughter and giggling.* **LADY HERTFORD** *is on the floor, laughing.*

FLUNKY Mr Justice Abbott and Lord Ellenborough.

PRINCE REGENT We were just playing spillikins! Lady Hertford was attempting to draw her stick from the bottom of the pile but unfortunately the entire structure has collapsed upon the floor...as indeed has Lady Hertford.

LORD ELLENBOROUGH Good evening, Your Ladyship.

LADY HERTFORD Why do you look so thunderous? Does the Lord Chief Justice disapprove of spillikins?

LORD ELLENBOROUGH No, madam. But no one likes to be the bearer of bad news. Justice Abbott, could you inform His Majesty of the latest developments in the Guildhall?

JUSTICE ABBOTT I am afraid Mr. Hone has been acquitted of blasphemous libel.

PRINCE REGENT Good God! How on earth did that happen? You promised me he was as good as on his way to the colonies... How did the people react to this outrage.

JUSTICE ABBOTT They laughed, Your Highness.

LORD ELLENBOROUGH It is the manner in which the mob express their vulgar joy.

PRINCE REGENT What have they got to be happy about? This man is a traitor to their monarch who they should love. He has ridiculed their prince and sought to foment rebellion throughout the kingdom.

JUSTICE ABBOTT Unfortunately we did not have sufficient evidence, sire.

PRINCE REGENT Damn your evidence. When I opened Parliament the mob attacked me with stones...

LADY HERTFORD ...I thought it was dung, Georgie?

PRINCE REGENT The fact is that they attacked the royal personage and this man Hone made light of it in his publication. Isn't that evidence enough?

LORD ELLENBOROUGH I agree, sire. The man is a menace to us all. He has undermined the judicial system trying to prove the innocence of the blasted Fenning girl...he's been meddling in the madhouses, demanding better treatment for lunatics, and he has even called for universal suffrage, a vote for every common man in the country...

PRINCE REGENT Which proves...he is a lunatic himself!

Everyone laughs politely.

LADY HERTFORD Most witty, Georgie!

PRINCE REGENT Yes, I thought so.

LORD ELLENBOROUGH ...which is why we cannot allow him to resume his campaign of what he calls "reform" and I call "revolution"!

LADY HERTFORD *squeals in horror.*

PRINCE REGENT Please, Lord Ellenborough. You must remember Lady Hertford's sensitivities.

LORD ELLENBOROUGH *(through gritted teeth)* My sincere apologies.

Enter **LADY CONYNGHAM.**

LADY CONYNGHAM Oh. I told my husband I had been summoned for spillikins. This doesn't look like spillikins.

PRINCE REGENT No. I have been badly let down by my counsellors and the insolent miscreant Hone remains free!

LADY CONYNGHAM How could this happen?

PRINCE REGENT *(to* **LORD ELLENBOROUGH***)* Yes, *how* could this happen?

LORD ELLENBOROUGH *looks in turn to* **JUSTICE ABBOTT.**

LORD ELLENBOROUGH Yes. How indeed could this happen?

PRINCE REGENT Hone was the wretch who published Cruikshank's drawing of my posterior likening it to a huge Spanish bomb!

LADY HERTFORD It's pronounced "Bum", Georgie.

PRINCE REGENT I know very well how it's pronounced...and so does damned Hone.

LADY CONYNGHAM And worse than that, the vile Cruikshank depicted somebody else's bum – which wasn't exactly small...

LADY HERTFORD *(sobbing)* This is what I have to put up with on your behalf...

She leaves the room.

LADY CONYNGHAM *(to* **LADY HERTFORD***)* I meant in the picture, dearest!

She leaves after her in fake concern.

PRINCE REGENT *(to* **LORD ELLENBOROUGH** *and* **JUSTICE ABBOTT***)* There! I hope you are satisfied, gentlemen, you have thoroughly ruined my game of spillikins! So what do you propose to do about it?

Scene Thirteen

HONE*'s home.* HONE *and* CRUIKSHANK *enter from the pub. Food is laid out on a table.*

HONE *(calling off but quiet)* Sarah! Sarah! We have won! It's over!

CRUIKSHANK David has slain Goliath! The Philistines have been defeated. The walls of Jericho are tumbling down!

CRUIKSHANK *effects a toot on an imaginary trumpet.*

HONE Shush, George...the children will be asleep!

CRUIKSHANK Why? It's early! Get them up! To salute their triumphant father...like Gideon rising up the against the Midianites!

HONE Not sure that one actually works, George. Perhaps we should not have stayed so long. Sarah? Sarah?

SARAH *enters with a basket of washing.*

HONE *holds out his arms.*

My darling Sarah!

SARAH *puts the basket of washing in his arms instead of herself and starts to fold it.*

SARAH So the victor returns...eventually. You were so long I thought perhaps I had been misinformed and you had gone to Australia.

CRUIKSHANK No! It was just the Southampton Arms!

HONE You're not helping, George.

CRUIKSHANK It was all my fault, Sarah. Such a great victory deserved a great celebration. No half measures!

SARAH So I can smell.

CRUIKSHANK *(very merry)* Don't be vexed. Your husband was astounding. His eloquence swept all before him. His wit and his powers of argument dazzled the jury. He was William the Conqueror, the game cock of Guildhall...

HONE Really, George...

CRUIKSHANK I shall draw you taking on the big wig and triumphing over the donkey-headed judge. Perhaps with a bulldog representing England cocking its leg to piss all over the prime minister.

HONE Really, George, there is a lady present...

CRUIKSHANK Sorry!

HONE You shouldn't mention the prime minister in polite society.

SARAH *at last laughs.*

SARAH I never doubted that your goodness would triumph.

HONE I did.

SARAH *laughs and pecks him on the cheek which turns into a proper kiss.* CRUICKSHANK *looks at the two of them.*

CRUIKSHANK Perhaps I should leave you two alone...although that does look like supper...

He sits down at the table. There is a bang on the door.

OFFICER *(offstage)* Open up!

SARAH Who is it?

OFFICER An officer from Justice Abbott! Open up at once!

SARAH *opens the door.*

SARAH Dear God, what can you want at this hour?

OFFICER I have a summons for William Hone!

SARAH There must be some mistake.

OFFICER There is not.

HONE What is it?

OFFICER William Hone, you are hereby charged with the offence of blasphemy...

CRUIKSHANK They can't do that! They just lost!

OFFICER ...and also with the *further* offence of seditious libel upon the person of the Prince Regent.

SARAH For pity's sake! Not a second trial surely? This is an outrage! Shame on you! Get out of my house!

HONE *(trying to calm* SARAH *down)* The officer is not responsible for this decision. I doubt he is an expert in the laws of defamation. You must save your anger for my accusers.

SARAH This is persecution!

OFFICER The law is of a different opinion.

HONE We have nothing to fear. I will prepare my case with the same rigour and meticulous attention to legal precedent as I did previously.

OFFICER Good luck with that. The trial of the King versus William Hone will come before the court at half past nine o'clock...tomorrow morning!

End of Act One

ACT TWO

Scene One

Courtroom. CRUIKSHANK *and* HONE *are sotto voce in court.*

CRUIKSHANK The crowd is even bigger today, William. There must be thousands! The Guildhall has never seen so many people. I could barely get in.

HONE The public enjoy a good hanging.

CRUIKSHANK No, you had the court in the palm of your hand. Today will be a walk in the park...without the ducks...and the drunkards and the prostitutes...

HONE A charming picture. But I appreciate your confidence in me.

CRUIKSHANK *(points to* HONE's *books of parodies)* Look at all these books. No one is going to be able to resist the tracts of Lord Somers!

HONE *(upbeat despite his misgivings)* He was a notable lawyer, and I shall argue that when the Law itself engages in parody it must be legal...

CRUIKSHANK An excellent argument, William. Throw in a couple of bumfiddle jokes, brown-nose the jury and you'll be free by teatime.

HONE *sighs.*

HONE Really, George. *(pause)* Mr Justice Abbott is late. Why is he late? What does that signify?

CRUIKSHANK Perhaps they have reviewed the merits of the case against you and decided to give up with this maggot in the head. Perhaps they have realised their folly and abandoned their vendetta against the free press...

CLERK All stand for the judge!

CRUIKSHANK ...or perhaps not.

LORD ELLENBOROUGH *enters and sits instead of* JUSTICE ABBOTT.

HONE Dear God – it's Ellenborough!

CLERK The Lord Chief Justice Abbott is indisposed. Lord Ellenborough will be presiding today.

CRUIKSHANK I don't believe it! He's given Abbott the boot. Ellenborough has taken over as judge!

HONE *(His mood is crushed.)* And jury no doubt!

LORD ELLENBOROUGH Silence in court!

CLERK The case of the King versus William Hone who is charged with impious and profane libel and also with seditious libel against the Prince Regent, the House of Lords and the House of Commons.

Mutterings of displeasure from CROWD.

LORD ELLENBOROUGH Are the sheriffs here?

CLERK They are not, My Lord.

LORD ELLENBOROUGH Then let them be immediately sent for. I am in charge today and I will have no disorder in my court. The Attorney General Sir Samuel Shepherd will proceed with the case for the prosecution.

SIR SHEPHERD Gentlemen of the jury, the heinous libel in question is a parody of that part of the divine service established by law called the Litany. You will recall that the Litany is a devout and heartfelt supplication to the Almighty which includes the passage "Son of God, we beseech thee to hear us. Oh lamb of god that takest away the sins of the world have mercy upon us." The defendant has turned this to ridicule. It is too disgusting to read his parody in its entirety.

MAN IN CROWD Shame!

LORD ELLENBOROUGH whips his head round to search for the heckler. HONE leaps to his feet and recites his litany before they can stop him.

HONE "Son of George, we beseech thee to hear us, Oh House of Lords that takest away so may thousands of pounds in pensions have mercy upon us!" *many?*

Huge laugh in court.

LORD ELLENBOROUGH *(very angrily)* Silence, Mr Hone! Where are the sheriffs?

SHERIFF *enters.*

SHERIFF We are here, My Lord.

LORD ELLENBOROUGH I have sent for you as there is an absolute necessity for your presence. I understand there were most unseemly disturbances in the court yesterday which will not be repeated today. You will apprehend any persons who dare to interrupt the course of these proceedings.

SHERIFF I assure Your Lordship that we will put a stop to any disgraceful or indecent conduct.

Murmur of dissent.

LORD ELLENBOROUGH Mr Hone, do you have *any* defence against the Attorney General's charges?

HONE Members of the jury, I am innocent of the charges and I will prove my case by referring to the historical precedents of parody, by reverent, distinguished and sober men of letters. These include the well known publication The Book of Chronicles of Westminster which contains scriptural parodies of the Westminster Elections which are clearly not designed to undermine religion but...

LORD ELLENBOROUGH I should warn you Mr Hone, that if you are going to argue that the scriptures have been ridiculed before by other persons then I shall not hear it. Crimes committed by other persons do not excuse yours. I declare such evidence as judicially inadmissible.

Shock and disapproval in court.

HONE Does Your Lordship intend to send me to prison without a fair trial?

More murmuring of dissent.

If Your Lordship does not mean that then you will allow me to make my defence to the jury.

Approval from CROWD. HONE *is now fighting for his life.*

LORD ELLENBOROUGH You are of course entitled to make your defence.

HONE I do not understand Your Lordship. If I am not permitted to read these publications to the jury I *have* no defence and you might as well dispense with all pretence of justice and send this poor bookseller to rot in a dungeon!

LORD ELLENBOROUGH This can have no reference to your case. The jury as sensible men must see that it has not.

HONE My Lord, I understand your notion of sensible men very well. What Your Lordship means by calling the jury sensible men is that they will find me guilty.

Laughter.

My notion of sensible men is that they will acquit me.

More laughter.

LORD ELLENBOROUGH Enough, Mr Hone! For the sake of demonstrating the even-handedness of justice I *will* hear you. However immaterial your contribution and however little good what you have to say will do you.

HONE I repeat, My Lord, that the object of the publication of the litany was a political one. I merely used the language of the Church because it is familiar to the vast majority of the people. There was no intention to bring religion into contempt.

LORD ELLENBOROUGH The intention is not the issue – it is the effect!

Murmurs of disapproval.

HONE The effect was to provoke laughter, My Lord. Laughter at our rulers. And that was always my intention...

Cut to:

Scene Two

Flashback. The clock spins backwards, lights fade up into a tavern.

A vulgar ballad is sung by a **FEMALE REVELLER.**

FEMALE REVELLER
COME PRICK UP YOUR EARS AND ATTEND, SIRS, AWHILE,

I'LL SING YE A SONG THAT SHALL MAKE YE TO SMILE,

'TIS A FAITHFUL DESCRIPTION OF THE TREE OF LIFE

SO PLEASING TO EVERY MAID, WIDOW AND WIFE...

CRUIKSHANK More! More!

HONE You always liked a low ballad, didn't you, George?

CRUIKSHANK No no. This is about the Tree of Life. From the Book of Genesis.

FEMALE REVELLER
THIS TREE UNIVERSAL MOST COUNTRIES PRODUCE

BUT TILL EIGHTEEN YEARS GROWTH 'TIS NOT MUCH FIT FOR USE,

THEN NINE OR TEN INCHES FOR IT SELDOM GROWS HIGHER

AND THAT'S SURE AS MUCH AS THE HEART CAN DESIRE.

Rowdy cheers.

CRUIKSHANK You see, it's basically a theological conceit.

FEMALE REVELLER
WE LADIES WHO LONG FOR A SIGHT OF THIS TREE

AWAIT INVITATION THIS WONDER TO SEE,

WE'D LIKE IT JUST NOW IN THE HEIGHT OF PERFECTION,

ADAPTED FOR HANDLING AND FIT FOR INJECTION.

Huge cheers at end of song.

HAZLITT *arrives to cast a pall.*

HAZLITT Very elevating, I am sure...

CRUIKSHANK Innocent fun, and based on the scriptures! Positively educational.

HAZLITT Really? I'd be careful with using the Bible for humorous effect if I were you.

HONE Nonsense, William!

HAZLITT It'll get you banished to Australia. It's a perfect excuse for the likes of Ellenborough. These are dangerous times.

HONE Comforting words, as ever.

CRUIKSHANK Though Australia isn't the *worst* place to be... apart from the poisonous snakes and spiders as big as soup bowls. And the heat, flies and natives, obviously.

HAZLITT Yes, I suppose, and it's true that travel makes a wise man better – and a fool worse. So don't worry – you have nothing to fear from Australia.

HONE That's good to hear, William.

HAZLITT The voyage out there will kill you soon enough so you'll never have to set foot in the godforsaken hellhole.

HONE Well, that's a relief.

HAZLITT I am merely being realistic. The perils of such a journey are well known... Quite apart from the possibility of scurvy or shipwreck you will be surrounded by hardened criminals... murderers and thieves who would happily slit you from head to toe for a bite of your weevil-ridden biscuit. No, your chances of surviving the passage would be extremely remote.

HONE *(to HAZLITT)* William, you have the unerring ability to lower the spirits.

HAZLITT I am merely pointing out the dangers of works such as your parody Litany.

CRUIKSHANK What's wrong with our litany?

HONE It is obviously a political litany, diligently revised, to be sung reverently by what our rulers call "the swinish multitude" throughout the taverns in the land.

HAZLITT That's what worries me.

HONE *(chants)*
OH PRINCE RULER OF THE PEOPLE, HAVE MERCY UPON US,
THY MISERABLE SUBJECTS.

CRUIKSHANK *(chants in response)*
OH GEORGE, HAVE MERCY UPON US.

HONE *(chants)*
GOOD PRINCE DELIVER US FROM A PARLIAMENT CHOSEN
ONLY BY ONE TENTH OF THE TAXPAYERS.

CRUIKSHANK *(chants)*
OH GEORGE, HAVE MERCY UPON US.

HONE *(chants)*
GOOD PRINCE, DELIVER US FROM ALL THE DEADLY SINS
ATTENDANT ON CORRUPT ELECTIONS AND ALL THE DECEITS
OF THE HIRELINGS OF THE PRESS, FROM JAILS CROWDED WITH
DEBTORS AND POORHOUSES OVERFLOWING WITH PAUPERS...

CRUIKSHANK *(chants exaggeratedly)*
OH GEORGE, HAVE MERCY UPON US!

HONE *(laughing)* And what about the Grace? We can't end without a Grace?

CRUIKSHANK *(singing)*
THE GRACE OF OUR LORD GEORGE, THE PRINCE REGENT,
AND THE LOVE OF LOUIS THE EIGHTEENTH OF FRANCE,
AND THE FELLOWSHIP OF THE POPE BE WITH US NOW AND
EVERMORE.

Even **HAZLITT** *laughs and joins in an elaborate three part harmony "AMEN".*

HONE, CRUIKSHANK *and* **HAZLITT**
A-A-A-MEN.

Cheers in pub fade out.

Scene Three

*Flash forward to present. We are back in the Guildhall
as* CLERK *reads out the passage they have just sung.*

CLERK ...and the fellowship of the Pope be with us now and
evermore. Amen.

CROWD *laughs and we hear a shout of "Amen".*

LORD ELLENBOROUGH I will have order in court! It is my
opinion that if this publication produces such an effect on
the minds of those who hear and read it then it *is* a libel.

HONE Then all I can say, gentlemen of the jury, is that *that* is
merely His Lordship's opinion.

LORD ELLENBOROUGH *(exploding)* It is *not* merely my opinion,
it is the opinion of all lawyers in all ages. The law says if
the publication has the tendency to inflame then the author
had the *intention* to inflame. No judge ever held differently.

HONE And that is Your Lordship's opinion. Which is but the
opinion of one man. His Lordship presides in this court but
you, the jury are my judges and to you I willingly submit
my case. *(cheekily)* And of course by this I mean no offence
to His Lordship.

Cheers of approval and laughter.

LORD ELLENBOROUGH Sheriffs! I instruct you to take into
custody any person who makes a disturbance!

More laughter.

SHERIFF The first man I see laugh I shall arrest him.

There is silence, then a few sniggers.

You there? Was that you laughing?

MAN IN CROWD No, sir. Not me, sir.

Others in CROWD *laugh at this.*

SHERIFF Who was that? Who dares to laugh?

Quite a lot of people are laughing now.

LORD ELLENBOROUGH Let the sheriffs bring any man before me and I will soon put an end to this insolent foolery.

More commotion in court.

Sheriff, have you taken any of the offenders?

SHERIFF No, My Lord, we have not succeeded.

LORD ELLENBOROUGH *(exasperated)* Open your eyes and look! Stretch out your hands and seize someone!

More laughter.

Clear the court! Clear the court!

Uproar and tumult.

Scene Four

We are outside the court. CRUIKSHANK *is having a smoke on a clay pipe while order is being restored in court.*

CRUIKSHANK You've *really* annoyed Ellenborough now.

HONE You think so?

CRUIKSHANK But at least everyone's still laughing.

HONE The men with the muskets weren't laughing. They seemed to have missed the joke.

CRUIKSHANK Never have I seen such an outrageous display of judicial prejudice and legal bias. Ellenborough is a disgrace to the bench.

HONE You did once draw him stamping on the British Press as the government lynched the figure of Liberty.

CRUIKSHANK Ah "Liberty Suspended". Very popular.

HONE But not with Lord Ellenborough – and probably hasn't helped us greatly today. It's been two hours. The Jury must be divided.

CRUIKSHANK No William you are like a brave Tom Tit , twitting the turkeys of the Law. Twit twit twittle twit. I shall draw the jury as fine cockerels crowing your victory.

Enter HAZLITT.

HAZLITT How brilliantly perceptive.

CRUIKSHANK Come down from your ivory tower have you Hazlitt?

HAZLITT Is it all over? Have I missed all the fun? You appear *not* to be in Australia.

HONE A temporary adjournment, William, while Ellenborough considers the practicalities of arresting a thousand people for unlawful merriment.

HAZLITT Then I must come in and offer you my support. There could be a column in it.

A **MR SOUTHALL** *approaches nervously.*

SOUTHALL Excuse me, sirs, but would you be the famous Mr Hazlitt?

HAZLITT Who wants to know?

SOUTHALL My name is Southall, sir. The gentleman in the tavern said you'd be here. I have travelled from Portsmouth in the hope of meeting you and witnessing your legendary scorn and caustic wit.

HAZLITT Then you are a clumpish addlepate of the first order!

SOUTHALL So scornful! So witty!

HAZLITT Wit is overrated. It is the salt of conversation, not the food.

SOUTHALL Thank you, sir, you have made my journey worthwhile.You are indeed the most original and contrary mind in London.

CRUIKSHANK You think so? Hardly. Like everyone else in the city, Hazlitt assumes that Hone here is going to lose his trial. An opinion shared by every lady's maid and butcher's boy in the capital. Original my bumshanks!

HAZLITT My friend Mr Cruikshank is of course wrong in his assumption, as he is in most matters. I have changed my mind. I consider William perfectly capable of overcoming impossible odds and triumphing over his enemies. If you think you can win, you can win. Faith is necessary to victory.

SOUTHALL Oh that's very, very good! So well phrased! May I buy you a drink?

CRUIKSHANK Of course.

SOUTHALL Not you – the celebrated Mr Hazlitt.

CRUIKSHANK I could do a drawing of you with Mr Hazlitt.

HAZLITT You will do no such thing. Excuse me, gentlemen, while I deal with the onerous duties of unlooked-for fame. Good luck, William.

HAZLITT *shakes his hand sincerely, and leaves with* **SOUTHALL.**

CRUIKSHANK Unlooked for? Nobody has looked for fame harder than William Hazlitt. Writer, critic, painter, philosopher, polemicist, biographer, social commentator, essayist...

HONE A little harsh George, but it is true that dear William is perhaps the least shrinking of the violet family.

CRUIKSHANK He has only one rule – that he will only write about anything, for anyone. Yet at the same time attacking the pimps and hirelings of the press! His pleasure in hating extends to everyone except you!

HONE A man of great taste and sound judgement. And when it comes to his dealings with his adoring public, I admire his patience.

CRUIKSHANK Nonsense. Pure vanity. Vanitas vanitatum!

HONE Just because the fellow didn't want your cartoon....

CLERK *interrupts them.*

CLERK The court is in session, Mr Hone.

Scene Five

Back in court. **LORD ELLENBOROUGH** *bangs his gavel to restore court to quiet.*

SHERIFF Order has been restored, Your Lordship.

LORD ELLENBOROUGH I would remind all those gathered here and outside the courtroom that they are risking contravening Lord Sidmouth's Seditious Meetings Act and his Treasonable Practices Bill.

CRUIKSHANK Is this a treasonable practice, William?

HONE No, I thought we were getting rather good at it.

LORD ELLENBOROUGH What was that, Mr Hone? Perhaps you would like to share your observations with the court?

HONE I was just saying, My Lord, that this disruption is most regrettable. I can assure you that none of my friends would take part in such mockery.

Laughter.

But I would urge all the good persons here to allow me to finish my defence against what are very serious charges. For not only am I on trial for libelling the scriptures but also for libelling the Prince Regent, the House of Lords and the House of Commons. Now, I do not expect gentlemen of the jury to share my political opinions but I do expect them to respect them, as I respect theirs.

Murmurs of approval.

In my political litany I tell the truth as I see it and a government which cannot hear the truth must be a despotism. That the jails are crowded with debtors, or that the poor houses are overflowing with paupers or that parliaments are not chosen by more than one tenth of the people are indisputable facts. If required I could go through every supplication in the litany to show that what I said was true and not libellous.

LORD ELLENBOROUGH That is *not* required, Mr Hone.

HONE Politics is my crime, pure and simple and the real libellers are those who instituted this hypocritical prosecution against me, which is aimed at nothing less than the liberty of the press. I am referring of course to the ministers of this government...

LORD ELLENBOROUGH ...who, I might remind the court, have been elected democratically...

HONE But have they? And by whom? Members of the jury may have seen my publication The Reformists' Register...

LORD ELLENBOROUGH I very much doubt they are readers of tuppeny trash...

HONE Well then perhaps I may familiarise them with the contents. In one edition I reported on Gatton in Surrey, a borough of six houses which returned two Members of Parliament.

The **CROWD** *shows disapproval.*

Those two members were Sir Mark Wood and his son. Sir Mark is the freeholder of all six houses, which means that there is only one elector in the borough. Sir Mark. Who voted for himself and his son.

LORD ELLENBOROUGH Sir Mark is well respected and much beloved in the borough!

HONE There are certainly not many people to tell him otherwise.

Laughter in court.

LORD ELLENBOROUGH This has nothing to do with parody.

HONE Your Lordship is correct. It is beyond parody. It is true.

More laughter.

And the truth is that if there is ridicule in my work it is because government ministers have rendered themselves ridiculous. Yes, I intended to laugh at them and laugh at them I will until they cease to be objects of my laughter by ceasing to be ministers. I ask you, is laughter treason? Surely not! Gentlemen of the jury, I may cut a wretched figure but I do not seek mercy. No, I seek justice!

Huge cheers from CROWD.

LORD ELLENBOROUGH *(less confident)* Members of the jury In obedience to my conscience and my God I pronounce this to be a most impious and profane libel. As Christians I have no doubt that you will be of the same opinion.

CLERK The jury will retire to reach its verdict.

Scene Six

Royal Appartments. Pompous Handel music. The royals are playing buffy gruffy, a parlour game which is essentially blind man's buff. PRINCE REGENT *is blindfolded and spun round by* LADY HERTFORD, THE DUKE OF YORK *and* LADY CONYNGHAM.

PRINCE REGENT I'm coming to get you...

LADY HERTFORD This way, Georgie!

DUKE OF YORK The whole point of Buffy Gruffy is that you're meant to try and escape...

LADY CONYNGHAM Over here, Georgie...

LADY HERTFORD Here I am...

DUKE OF YORK No, you're making it too easy for him...

LADY HERTFORD Don't be such a spoilsport, Freddie!

> PRINCE REGENT *stumbles around, and nearly grabs* FLUNKY. *The women squeal with delight.*

LADY CONYNGHAM Getting warmer...

PRINCE REGENT I'm getting very hot indeed...

> *He lunges at* LADY CONYNGHAM *but gets* DUKE OF YORK *from behind by mistake.*

Gotcha!

The two ladies squeal.

Now who can it be...

PRINCE REGENT *feels his brother's posterior...*

Unmistakably the Venus of St James...or perhaps it is Albion's Aphrodite come down to our mortal realm...

DUKE OF YORK Get off, George, you prize clodpole!

PRINCE REGENT *removes his blindfold.*

PRINCE REGENT Oh. Disappointing! It's you.

Laughter from all except **DUKE OF YORK.**

DUKE OF YORK This is a damned silly game.

PRINCE REGENT Well, what would you rather play. Flapdragon?

DUKE OF YORK No.

LADY CONYNGHAM No, last time we played, Freddie's wig caught fire. It was jolly funny.

DUKE OF YORK No it wasn't.

PRINCE REGENT Yes it was, and don't argue, Freddie, because... *(He can't think of a reason.)* ...I'm the Regent.

LADY HERTFORD Oh! Georgie, you're *so* commanding!

PRINCE REGENT *(to* **FLUNKY***)* You there – fetch a bowl of flaming brandy and some raisins and plums. We are going to play flapdragon!

LADY CONYNGHAM Commanding but also decisive!

LADY HERTFORD You are going to make such a strong king!

PRINCE REGENT Yes, if only nature would take its course and relieve my poor father of the burdens of earthly existence.

DUKE OF YORK What he's saying is he wishes the mad old fool would hurry up and die.

PRINCE REGENT I was saying no such thing...though as heir it is somewhat tiresome to be kept waiting in the wings. Not being the actual king, even though one is quite old enough...

LADY CONYNGHAM ...and wise enough!

PRINCE REGENT Yes. Nothing to do but exert what little authority one has...and be mocked by the likes of Hone for doing one's best for the public good.

LADY CONYNGHAM Poor Georgie.

LADY HERTFORD Yes, poor, poor Georgie...

PRINCE REGENT No prince should ever endure such ignominy ever again. It really is...appalling.

Pause, then to **FLUNKY**, *who has been listening to this self-pitying whinge.*

Dammit man, where's that flaming brandy?

FLUNKY I'm sorry, sire...

FLUNKY bows and hastens to the door to be met head-on by **LORD ELLENBOROUGH** *and* **LORD SIDMOUTH**.

Ah. Lords Ellenborough and Sidmouth. How may I assist you?

LORD ELLENBOROUGH By getting out the damned way, you sapskull!

FLUNKY Your Majesty, Lords Ellenborough and Sidmouth desire an audience...

PRINCE REGENT Excellent. They are no doubt bringing me my Christmas present...namely William Hone in jail.

LADY CONYNGHAM Most amusing, Georgie.

LADY HERTFORD Yes, I thought so as well...first!

Enter **LORD ELLENBOROUGH** *and* **LORD SIDMOUTH**, *pushing* **FLUNKY** *out of the way. They are both clearly blaming each other for the latest failure.*

LORD ELLENBOROUGH Your Highnesses, ladies, I am sorry to interrupt your festive revels but I bring bad tidings. Hone has been acquitted...again.

PRINCE REGENT WHAT! You said you would see to it yourself that this time he was silenced for good! He would be muted by a display of strength! The triumph of the sledgehammer over the nut!

DUKE OF YORK What in thunderation went wrong?

LORD SIDMOUTH Lord Ellenborough was unable to persuade them to fulfil their duty as loyal subjects and upstanding Christians.

LORD ELLENBOROUGH Regrettably the jury were infected by the public mood of disaffection that Lord Sidmouth's administration has been unable to assuage!

PRINCE REGENT I don't give a fig for your excuses. This verdict is an outrage on almighty God and furthermore...

(shouts) on our royal self!

LORD ELLENBOROUGH *and* SIDMOUTH Indeed it is, sire.

PRINCE REGENT So what do we do now? What do you say, Lord Chief Justice?

LORD ELLENBOROUGH Well, clearly we try him again.

DUKE OF YORK Third time lucky, eh?

LORD SIDMOUTH I am not entirely sure that is a good idea, Your Majesty. Two acquittals from two juries would suggest that perhaps the law is not the most effective means of dealing with this matter.

LORD ELLENBOROUGH Nonsense. If the Home Secretary had seen to it that there were more officers to contain the Godless rabble, then perhaps the law would have been upheld!

LORD SIDMOUTH Merely continuing with the prosecution might make Your Majesty look vindictive...

PRINCE REGENT I will punish anyone who says I am vindictive!

The ladies both applaud this machismo.

LORD SIDMOUTH Indeed, sire. But perhaps a different tactic might bear fruit.

LADY CONYNGHAM I know, Georgie! Remember that miserable cartoonist Gillray? Didn't you give him a secret pension?

DUKE OF YORK Yes, Canning paid him off and he soon changed his tune. Whereas before he drew George as, what was it, a corpulent voluptuary?

PRINCE REGENT Thank you for reminding us, Freddie...

DUKE OF YORK ...he then stuck his pen into Bonaparte instead. In fact we paid him so much he could afford to drink himself to death. Only thing Gillray ever did that made me laugh. Haw haw!

LORD ELLENBOROUGH The matter of Gillray's "secret" pension was raised in open court. It did not help the case much.

LADY HERTFORD But if you paid off this man Hone, would he and his beastly friend Cruikshank stop portraying me as... shall we say, "well-rounded"?

LORD ELLENBOROUGH Your Ladyship, with respect, there are more weighty matters at stake here...

DUKE OF YORK You can't get much weightier than Lady Hertford!

LADY HERTFORD *(sobs)* How cruel you are, Freddie...

LADY CONYNGHAM Yes, Georgie, tell him to stop being so horrid about Lady Hertford's delightfully ample form!

PRINCE REGENT You have gone too far, sir!

DUKE OF YORK Forgive me, I meant no offence, Lady Hertford. I was merely agreeing with Lord Sidmouth that sometimes one *has* to endure this sort of snide wittling from the envious masses... I myself have been defamed in a scurrilous nursery rhyme accusing me of taking ten thousand men up a hill and then down again.

LADY HERTFORD Now that *was* funny.

DUKE OF YORK It was not funny, it was extremely unfortunate that my one field command in Flanders failed to achieve all the military objectives including the taking of the so-called hill which was actually a fortified town and...

PRINCE REGENT Yes all right, Freddie. We have all heard this before...

LORD SIDMOUTH Perhaps a strategic retreat might be efficacious in this matter also, Your Highness? Perhaps we should avoid further humiliation and postpone the third trial?

LORD ELLENBOROUGH Have you lost your backbone, Sidmouth? Has this upstart bookseller knocked the stuffing out of His Majesty's government?

PRINCE REGENT Gentlemen, gentlemen, no raised voices please. If we are not united then the likes of Hone will have succeeded.

LORD ELLENBOROUGH But there are important matters to decide. What are we going to do now?

LADY HERTFORD *strikes a theatrical pose.*

LADY HERTFORD Charades?

Scene Seven

HONE's *house, night. The front room is empty. We hear banging. Bang on door. Nobody answers.*

OFFICER *(offstage)* Mr Hone! Mr Hone! I must speak with you.

More banging.

Mr Hone, I am an officer of the law. You must open the door.

HONE *enters in a nightshirt, very groggy.*

HONE What is it?

HONE *opens door to reveal* OFFICER. *It is snowing outside.*

OFFICER I'm sorry to disturb you, Mr Hone...but I am here on official business.

Enter SARAH, *who's angry.*

SARAH For pity's sake, the poor man's half-dead with exhaustion. Can it wait until morning?

OFFICER It cannot.

SARAH Shame on you for a dragging an ill man from his bed!

HONE *(devastated)* I don't believe it... You have come with another summons from Lord Ellenborough.

OFFICER I'm afraid so, sir.

HONE And what is the charge to be this time?

OFFICER William Hone, you are required by the court to present yourself to the Guildhall tomorrow morning at nine o'clock, to be tried for publishing an irreligious and profane libel on the Athanasian Creed!

SARAH For pity's sake! Not a third trial surely? Has anyone ever endured three trials in three days?

HONE *(wilting visibly)* I do not know if I can carry on.

SARAH I know you, William, you will find the strength.

HONE What little strength I have left comes from you. Without your support I would have succumbed to despair many years since. But I am not sure I can face the ordeal for a third time.

SARAH This is madness. Why will the government not abandon this absurd and disgraceful vendetta against my husband? You, sir, should be ashamed of yourself, for your part in this persecution of an honest, blameless man!

OFFICER That is as maybe, but Mr Hone's presence is required at the Guildhall tomorrow morning.

HONE I can't do it.

OFFICER You should have left the country when you had the chance, Mr Hone. Fled to America like your friend William Cobbett.

(pause, then surreptitiously) There is still time...you are not yet in custody.

SARAH *(furious)* No, sir! My husband is *not* William Cobbett! He is not scuttling off like a frightened rat to become a fugitive, leaving his wife and family behind...

HONE *(placatory)* I think the officer meant well, Sarah...

SARAH You don't know my husband if you imagine he is the coward to desert a cause he believes to be right! He is not going to *escape* justice – he is going to *demand* justice!

HONE Whoever this paragon of valour you are describing is, I would certainly like to meet him. Perhaps he could inspire me with some of his courage and resolve.

SARAH Believe me, he is an inspiration to all who meet him. Even, apparently, his wife.

HONE *smiles.*

OFFICER *turns to leave.*

HONE Officer, it must be cold out there, would you come into the warm and have a drink?

OFFICER Well, thank you, sir...

SARAH One day, William, your generosity will be your undoing!

HONE But it is Christmas, which is the season of goodwill, even if no one has informed Lord Ellenborough.

Scene Eight

Courtroom. Buzz of CROWD. CRUIKSHANK *is in his familiar place, but there is no sign of* HONE. SARAH *has turned up for the last trial to give moral support.*

LORD ELLENBOROUGH *(less confident, croakier)* The proceedings are already half an hour late in commencing. Is there still no sign of the defendant?

SHERIFF No, My Lord. And the mob is even larger and more unruly than yesterday.

LORD ELLENBOROUGH Then summon more men.

CRUIKSHANK *(to* SARAH*)* Where is William?

SARAH I thought he was here with you...

SHERIFF *(to* ELLENBOROUGH*)* My Lord, I fear that however many men be summoned will be insufficient. I have estimates of twenty thousand awaiting the verdict outside the Guildhall.

LORD ELLENBOROUGH Twenty thousand? Dear God. Fetch however many officers as can be mustered and instruct the captain if necessary to call in the dragoons.

SHERIFF Are you serious, My Lord?

LORD ELLENBOROUGH I hope you are not questioning my judgement?

SHERIFF No, My Lord.

LORD ELLENBOROUGH There will be no riot when – and I mean when – Hone is found guilty.

SHERIFF Very good, My Lord.

He exits.

LORD ELLENBOROUGH Where is Mr Hone? It will certainly be easier to try him in his absence.

CRUIKSHANK He is indisposed, My Lord. He is not a well man.

LORD ELLENBOROUGH Then perhaps we have no other option but to commence proceedings whilst he is incapacitated. It would give me no greater satisfaction than to have this matter done with by luncheon. So if the defendant cannot appear for whatever reason, then I shall have no alternative but to accept his absence as a confession of guilt, and judge him accord—

HONE *appears, looking very ill indeed.*

(disappointed) Oh. You're here.

HONE I apologise profusely to the court and beg your forgiveness. I was attempting to assemble fresh evidence for my defence.

He sits down alongside CRUIKSHANK *and* SARAH.

LORD ELLENBOROUGH Well, that would be a novelty. Are you now ready to proceed?

HONE Just five minutes' grace, My Lord?

He attempts to organise his books some of which fall on the floor in disarray.

CRUIKSHANK *(encouragingly)* Here we go, old friend. Once more unto the breach.

SARAH Look at them, William. The people are behind you. They are willing you to win.

HONE Though Lord Ellenborough looks more determined than ever.

CRUIKSHANK You know his motto – If at first you don't succeed, try, try and try you again.

HONE *doesn't laugh.*

Are you all right, William? That was one of my better jokes. You are not yourself.

SARAH He is unwell.

HONE No, I am weary, George. Weary that I have to rehearse all my arguments again, for yet another jury who may not stand up to Ellenborough's browbeating so robustly. If only I had something new to say. I am sure there is something I have forgotten...something I read about about the Athanasian Creed...

SARAH Is there anything I can do?

HONE I am sure there is something in the shop amongst my papers...but I couldn't find it.

SARAH I am familiar with the inventory and in your absence have tried to catalogue all your books and restore some order...not an easy task.

HONE Anything about the creed...

They kiss, briefly. SARAH *leaves the court.*

LORD ELLENBOROUGH If you are ill, Mr Hone, you could ask for a postponement.

HONE No, I will make no such request.

LORD ELLENBOROUGH Mr Hone, you really do look most unwell.

HONE No, My Lord. I am not yet conveniently dead. I am glad to be here and very glad to see Your Lordship.

Laughter in court. This revives HONE. CLERK *bangs a staff to get silence.*

We *will* finish this today.

LORD ELLENBOROUGH So be it.

CLERK The case of the King against William Hone, bookseller and publisher, for publishing an irreligious and profane libel on that part of the divine service of the Church of England denominated the Athanasian Creed.

LORD ELLENBOROUGH Would the Attorney General state the prosecution's case?

SIR SHEPHERD Thank you, My Lord. I see from the number of books now upon Mr Hone's table that he is going to attempt to argue that merely because blasphemous libels have been committed in the past, he is currently at liberty to scandalise religion. This is not the law.

HONE *rises wearily to his feet.*

HONE I must dispute that...

LORD ELLENBOROUGH Sit down, Mr Hone, before you fall down. Let the Attorney General finish.

HONE *slumps into his seat.*

SIR SHEPHERD As members of the jury will know, as devout Christians, the Athanasian creed states our sacred belief in the Holy Trinity: The father, son and Holy Ghost. In Mr Hone's "Sinecurist's Creed" these divine elements of the Godhead become vulgar nicknames of Mr Hone's targets of ridicule: the Lord Chancellor, the Foreign Secretary and Lord Sidmouth.

A boo from **CROWD.**

As he writes in his disgraceful satire, "Glory Be to 'Old Bags', 'Derry Down Triangle' and to 'The Doctor'. As it was in the beginning, is now and ever shall be, without end, Amen."

Laughter, and cries of "Amen". Gavel banging.

LORD ELLENBOROUGH Does anyone understand the origin of these infantile soubriquets?

MAN IN CROWD *We* do!

Laughter. **SHEPHERD** *and* **LORD ELLENBOROUGH** *go into a huddle.*

SIR SHEPHERD *(sotto voce)* I think it better not to further Mr Hone's libels by giving them the dignity of an explanation.

LORD ELLENBOROUGH I'll be the judge of that.

SIR SHEPHERD *(confidentially to* LORD ELLENBOROUGH *)* "Old Bags" refers to the Chancellor's family money, which came from coal mines, "Derry Down Triangle" is a reference to Lord Castlereagh's alleged instrument of torture used in Ireland. And "the Doctor" refers to Lord Sidmouth's father, who ran a mad house...which would no doubt give Mr Hone the opportunity to coin witticisms about the Home Secretary also running an asylum for the insane. I think this would be most unwise.

LORD ELLENBOROUGH *(to court)* Sir Samuel is quite right. We need not further waste the court's time with this childish folderol.

The lights fade down on court. In a spotlight we see SARAH *searching desperately through a pile of books and papers on a desk. The office is a mass of papers. Behind her the clock is turning fast to indicate time passing. She opens a cupboard. More papers spew out. Lights fade down on* SARAH *and up on the court.*

Mr Hone, how do you answer the Attorney General's charges against you?

HONE I shall make it clear...

LORD ELLENBOROUGH ...and I shall not allow you to repeat your defence of literary precedent.

HONE *(seriously worried, at his wit's end)* Your Lordship, I sustained an injury from you yesterday, when Your Lordship interrupted me a great many times, and then said you would interrupt me no more. And then your lordship DID interrupt me, ten times as much as you'd done before, and...

Laughter and jeers.

LORD ELLENBOROUGH Mr Hone, I cannot sit here and be attacked!

HONE Your Lordship is interrupting me again!

Big laugh.

LORD ELLENBOROUGH Very well, you shall not be interrupted again and the jury can make what they will of your relentless, irrelevant and unconvincing historical lecture.

HONE *(searching through his bundles of documents)* Thank you. Now I shall turn to... Er, no, we've been there...er... Ah yes, let me refer now to Mr Walter Scott, whose recent work "Tales from My Landlord" abounds with scriptural phrases that are used absurdly by caricatured Scotsmen such as...

(puts on silly Scottish accent) Jebediah Cleishbotham of Gandercleugh...

Laughs from **CROWD.**

Yet we have not seen Mr Scott dragged in chains from Edinburgh...

Lights fade down on the court and up on **SARAH,** *still searching through* **HONE***'s papers for a pamphlet. She finds, under a pile of papers, a pisspot. She turns it upside down...dust and more papers pour out. Lights go down on* **SARAH** *and up on* **HONE.**

(holding up a print of Fuseli's Nightmare) ...and here we see the celebrated artist Mr Fusili parodying the Lord Mayor as a "Night" mare... *spelling ?*

Laughter and groans.

...a somewhat laboured pun, but effective in demonstrating once again, how...

LORD ELLENBOROUGH Mr Hone, I have been a model of restraint, but you have now been on your feet for some eight hours and appear to have quoted every parody you quoted yesterday and many, many more besides. I must insist that you reach a conclusion.

HONE My conclusion, Your Lordship is... *(desperately trying to waste time)* that there is an old saying that "experience makes fools wise". Yet if there was any truth in the proverb,

I would not be in court for the third time after twice being acquitted on similar charges!

Half-hearted cheers.

LORD ELLENBOROUGH I mean it, Mr Hone!

HONE *shuffles his books and searches his papers in desperation.*

Lights fade down on the court and up on **SARAH**, *still searching through* **HONE***'s papers for a pamphlet. Suddenly, she lets out a cry.*

She bends down and holds up not the pamphlet she's been searching for – but a dead rat. Lights go down on **SARAH** *and up on* **HONE**.

HONE Have I mentioned The Harleian Miscellany of 1647, particularly the second volume by Mr Dutton in which he parodies prayer...?

LORD ELLENBOROUGH You have indeed, at some length...

HONE Yes, I have. So, finally, to sum up, in conclusion, Gentlemen of the jury, taking all things into consideration...

HONE *is floundering.*

A cry from the gallery.

HECKLER Get on with it!

HONE *is losing the* **CROWD**.

LORD ELLENBOROUGH At last – a sensible interjection! Perhaps you could, as the gentleman said, "get on with it".

A laugh for **LORD ELLENBOROUGH**. **HONE** *is more flustered.*

HONE Indeed.

Pause, as he takes a breath and realises this is the last roll of the dice.

Members of the jury, I look to you for rescue from this bigoted prosecution. Upon my conscience, I had no more intention of ridiculing St Athanasius's creed than I have of murdering my wife and children when I get home.

SARAH *arrives. She looks triumphant. She is carrying some papers.*

(brighter) But I have no such intention, and as you can see my wife is alive and well.

Big laugh from **CROWD.**

My Lord, may we adjourn briefly?

LORD ELLENBOROUGH I hope you are not wasting the court's time, Mr Hone. Let me rephrase that – I hope you are not wasting *more* of the court's time.

SARAH *gives* **HONE** *the papers, and confers briefly. He searches through the papers and then grabs a book on the table to cross refer.*

SIR SHEPHERD I must protest. This is most irregular!

HONE Three trials in three days is most irregular.

LORD ELLENBOROUGH Please, Mr Hone, let us proceed...

HONE Members of the jury, thank you for your tolerance. *(***HONE*** resumes defence.)* I will now proceed to the crux of the matter. The prosecution call the Athanasian Creed "sacred". But some historians have argued that it was not written by St Athanasius at all – but it was, in fact, a *parody* of his creed written by someone four centuries later.

Gasps from the court.

Furthermore, many distinguished clergymen in recent times have doubted the very authenticity and sanctity of the creed, and wished to be rid of it.

SIR SHEPHERD Which clergymen? You must name names, Mr Hone!

HONE You desire names, sir?

SIR SHEPHERD Indeed I do. This court will not allow the libellers their usual trick of anonymity. Which supposedly distinguished clergymen have traduced this holy writ?

HONE Very well, sir. How about this for a name? The late Bishop of Carlisle, who you may know better as the father... of Lord Ellenborough!

Gasps from the court. Gavel banging.

Is that not correct, My Lord. Your own father was guilty of the supposed crime of which you accuse me?

SIR SHEPHERD I ask the questions in this court.

HONE Would you describe yourself as the son of a blasphemer? Would you send your own father to jail?

LORD ELLENBOROUGH *(weakly)* My poor father is long dead and has gone to a place where he will have to account for his opinions...

HONE But that place is not Australia, is it? And his judge is an even higher one than yourself?

SIR SHEPHERD You are not allowed to cross-examine the judge!

HONE I ask you again, Lord Ellenborough, did your father, the Bishop of Carlisle, the Master of Peterhouse Cambridge and Knightsbridge Professor of Philosophy, not believe that the Athanasian Creed was apocryphal?

LORD ELLENBOROUGH *(crushed)* For common decency, Mr Hone, please forbear!

HONE My Lord, I shall. Just as soon as we establish that your father, who by all accounts was a man of great softness of manners and who was accounted a great champion of Christian liberty...

LORD ELLENBOROUGH Yes, yes...

HONE ...was the author of pamphlets, including *anonymous* pamphlets, opposing the strict adherence to doctrine and in favour of religious toleration – pamphlets which I would be proud to publish today...

Cheers from **CROWD**.

LORD ELLENBOROUGH I think we have all heard enough about my late father!

HONE No, no, My Lord, I for one would like to hear a great deal more of your father's unorthodox theological views and his Whig politics, which may well conflict with your own...

Jeers from **CROWD**. *One voice is heard.*

MAN IN CROWD Same old Tory!

Laughs from **CROWD**.

HONE ...but I shall desist and in so doing I shall display the Christian forbearance that is so lamentably absent in my accusers.

LORD ELLENBOROUGH *(defeated)* Mr Hone, you have been addressing the court for an unprecedented length of time. Perhaps you would be so good as to bring your defence *finally* to a close?

HONE Gentlemen of the jury, I will say just this. Unlike many others, I have never written or printed what I did not think right or true. I have always acted for the public good, without regard to what other men did, however exalted their rank.

Cheers from the court.

The consciousness of my innocence gives me life, spirit and strength to go through this *third* ordeal of persecution and oppression. Gentlemen of the jury, the powers that be thought that a poor, oppressed man could not stand three days in court. They thought that their united force would crush me like an insect. But two juries of cool, honest Englishmen have already acquitted me. I have no doubt that you too, gentlemen of the jury, will send me home to dine on Sunday with my wife and children!

Huge applause. Cheers fade out. The clock moves forward.

Scene Nine

Courtroom. Gavel bang.

LORD ELLENBOROUGH Is the defendant present?

We do not see the defendant at this point. Focus is on **LORD ELLENBOROUGH.**

CLERK He is indeed, Your Lordship.

LORD ELLENBOROUGH I have given this case my full attention, and I have no alternative but to reach a right and proper verdict myself.

Gasps and boos from **CROWD.**

Having given your case my full consideration, I find you... *guilty!*

More boos, he bangs the gavel.

...and I have no hesitation in sentencing you accordingly. You are a threat to public order and have shown no remorse as to the damage incurred by your crime. I therefore have no alternative but to sentence you be detained in custody.

MAN IN CROWD Shame!

LORD ELLENBOROUGH ...and to remain incarcerated until you have paid a fine of twenty pounds.

More boos.

Does the defendant have anything to say for himself? Mr Weatherill, speak up!

Reveal it's not **HONE,** *but a young student,* **WEATHERILL,** *who is in the dock.*

WEATHERILL My Lord, I am a poor student who is innocent of the charge of riotous conduct. I was apprehended on the steps of the Guildhall... The marshal laid a hand on

my arm and I sought to defend myself. There was a scuffle.
I became betwattled! It was a misunderstanding! I was
merely trying to enter the court to hear the verdict on the
famous Mr Hone...

LORD ELLENBOROUGH Sheriff, take him away. And may that
be a lesson to everyone else!

Boos from **CROWD.**

Scene Ten

Courtroom. The clock whizzes forward. CLERK *bangs a staff.* SARAH, HONE *and* CRUIKSHANK *await the verdict.*

CLERK The jury has returned.

CRUIKSHANK They have only been out twenty minutes!

HONE Perhaps my last twenty minutes of liberty.

SARAH The last twenty minutes of liberty for us all!

LORD ELLENBOROUGH Foreman, have you reached a verdict?

FOREMAN We have.

LORD ELLENBOROUGH Is the defendant Mr William Hone guilty or not guilty?

Pause.

FOREMAN *(voice off) Not* guilty!

The court erupts. Cheers, applause, stamping etc.

Scene Eleven

Street atmosphere, cheering, chanting, sound of horses and carriages etc.

CRUIKSHANK Make way for the victor! Make way for the great William Hone! The Colossus of the Courts! The Lysander of Liberty!

HONE Really, George...you are prone to exaggeration...

CRUIKSHANK Of course I am! I'm a caricaturist!

Cheers. Rabble starts singing. **CRUIKSHANK** *joins in.*

SONG: "BIG WIG".

CROWD
HOW MAJESTIC IS LAW,
HOW IT SWELLS AND LOOKS BIG,
HOW TREMENDOUS ITS BROW
AND HOW AWFUL ITS WIG.
BUT THE THREE HONEST JURIES
DID NOT GIVE A FIG,
FOR THE FROWN OF THE JUDGE
IN HIS AWFUL BIG WIG.
OH THE THREE HONEST JURIES,
HUZZAH! HUZZAH! HUZZAH!

LORD ELLENBOROUGH *comes to centre stage and addresses the audience.*

LORD ELLENBOROUGH On my way home the jeering rabble followed me, but as my carriage passed Charing Cross, I told my driver to stop and I got out to buy some kippers for my supper! The rabble spat at me – but I laughed at the hooting and tumultuous mob. I was more afraid of their saliva than their bite.

PRINCE REGENT *takes centre stage amidst the singing and noise. He's draped in his bedclothes and holding a glass of wine.*

PRINCE REGENT *(quite sozzled)* When I heard the news that the damned bookseller had got away with it, I resolved to learn my lesson and mend my ways, and never again become the victim of vile opprobrium and ridicule...but still I was verry...what was it?

LADY HERTFORD *(popping up from underneath the bedclothes)* Cross, Georgie!

LADY CONYNGHAM *(also appears from underneath the bedclothes)* Very cross!

LADY HERTFORD Very, very cross!

LADY CONYNGHAM Very, very, very cross!

PRINCE REGENT Suffice to say...I was as cross as crabs!

Swigs wine and disappears under bedclothes with LADY HERTFORD *and* LADY CONYNGHAM.

CRUIKSHANK *is now centre stage, addressing the audience.*

CRUIKSHANK It was an historic and momentous day in the long, noble struggle for freedom – and I suggested we mark it appropriately...by getting nob-headingly tap-hackled, jug-bitten and ape-drunk as a wheelbarrow! But William just melted into the crowd.

(looking around, now in real time) William? William? Has anyone seen William Hone? William? I'm looking for William Hone. William?

(shouts above the din) WILLIAM!

CROWD *atmosphere. We hear the song again.*

CROWD

> PEOPLE SAY LAW IS SHARP
> AND IT CUTS THROUGH A STONE
> BUT THESE RECENT EVENTS
> MUST COMPEL THEM TO OWN
> THAT THE GALLANT BOOKSELLER
> WON THRICE ALL ALONE
> AND THE EDGE OF THE LAW
> WAS PROVED BLUNT ON A HONE.
> OH THE THREE HONEST JURIES,
> HUZZAH! HUZZAH! HUZZAH!

It then fades to be replaced by toll of church bell.

Scene Twelve

Churchyard. Torrential rain. A church bell tolls.
Mourners appear and move on including **SARAH,** *dressed*
in black and distraught.

A **MOURNER** *in a stovepipe hat is stopped by a* **CUB**
REPORTER.

CUB REPORTER Sir, forgive me. I have been instructed by my
editor to report on this funeral. Can you tell me something
of the deceased?

MOURNER We are mourning the death of William Hone.

CUB REPORTER Who?

MOURNER William Hone. Publisher, satirist, campaigner
for universal suffrage, investigative reporter, inspector of
asylums, philanthropist...

CUB REPORTER Please, sir, you are going too fast, I can't get
it all down...

MOURNER Perhaps I should write it for you? Hone was probably
the most important man in the annals of press freedom.
You must have heard of his trials?

CUB REPORTER When were they, sir?

MOURNER Some twenty-five years ago.

CUB REPORTER Before I was born. No wonder I have never
heard of him.

MOURNER Ah, the ignorance of youth. Hone had his moment
but obscurity beckoned.

CUB REPORTER Is there anyone famous attending?

MOURNER See the red-faced man over there talking to the
widow and looking preposterous in a ludicrous waistcoat?
That's the great artist George Cruikshank.

CUB REPORTER Really?

MOURNER Once he was a ferocious and acerbic cartoonist. Of course, that was before he accepted a handsome pension from the late king and turned into a respectable illustrator.

CUB REPORTER I don't understand, sir.

MOURNER Such is life. But old Cruikshank can still raise a laugh – don't you think his unruly whiskers give him the appearance of a bedraggled bird's nest?

CUB REPORTER *(sniggers)* Yes, they do! Did he know Mr. Hone well?

MOURNER They were the greatest of friends. He may be a model of sobriety now but Cruikshank sponged off poor old Hone shamelessly in his drinking and whoring days.

CRUIKSHANK *overhears this conversation and butts in. He is twenty-five years older, looking somewhat bedraggled.*

CRUIKSHANK *(offstage)* What's that, sir?

MOURNER *(speaking up)* I was talking of your thinking and drawing days, George. Sadly long past!

CRUIKSHANK Height of my powers, sir!

MOURNER *(to SARAH)* My condolences, Mrs Hone.

SARAH Thank you, sir. My family is bereft at our loss, but thankfully I have the support of my...ten children.

CUB REPORTER Ten?!

SARAH My husband was most productive in all his endeavours.

MOURNER Indeed. It is a sad day, George, is it not?

CRUIKSHANK It is. So why are you smirking, sir?

MOURNER *is indeed trying to suppress a smirk.*

MOURNER I couldn't help witnessing your altercation with Reverend Binney.

SARAH Yes, George, why did you threaten to punch the good Reverend's head? You no longer have the excuse of being drunk! Do you owe him money?

MOURNER *gets the giggles again. As does* SARAH, *despite her grief.*

CRUIKSHANK *(very pompously)* How could you think such a thing, Sarah? No, the Reverend was very rude about a tribute I wrote to William.

SARAH Perhaps you should take him to court!

CRUIKSHANK What?

CUB REPORTER *(to* MOURNER*)* So what were your memories of the deceased? Preferably short ones.

MOURNER My abiding memory is of how much he made us laugh – and how he finished off old Ellenborough at the trial.

CRUIKSHANK Yes, he never sat as a judge again. Died within the year. Nobody mourned *him!*

MOURNER And of course it was Ellenborough who refused Eliza Fenning's appeal...

SARAH Oh yes, the Fenning girl! William was right about her all along.

CUB REPORTER Who was the Fenning girl?

MOURNER You'll like this – the case had everything a proper journalist could wish for – an unjust hanging, poison, licentiousness and dumplings...

CUB REPORTER *(perks up)* Ah, dumplings!

He stars scribbling.

SARAH It was all a long time ago but my dear husband was very exercised by it, and I should never have doubted him.

CRUIKSHANK *(to* CUB REPORTER*)* It turned out the brother of Eliza's master was a lunatic – and he died in a workhouse, confessing to the poisoning.

MOURNER It was all in The Times. She was finally proved innocent. All thanks to William.

CUB REPORTER Hmm...useful background but I really need some more tributes. Mr Cruikshank, how will you remember Mr. Hone?

CRUIKSHANK I regret to say that due to my past lack of temperance regarding the demon drink I cannot remember all the detail of our time together, but I do know that William Hone was the bravest champion in our hour of need.

CUB REPORTER Can I quote you on that, sir?

MOURNER *(to* **CUB REPORTER***)* Of course you can!

You owe your liberty to report the truth unfettered, to William Hone's noble stand against the might of a corrupt government.

Church bell tolls.

Come, George, Mrs Hone, it is time to pay our last respects.

CUB REPORTER Sir – before you go – your name, sir?

MOURNER Dickens. Charles Dickens. Good day.

CUB REPORTER *looks to the heavens and slaps his head.*

CUB REPORTER Oh!

Ends

After the curtain call, the cast all sing:

SONG: "BIG WIG" – REPRISE.

CAST
PEOPLE SAY LAW IS SHARP
AND IT CUTS THROUGH A STONE,
BUT THESE RECENT EVENTS
MUST COMPEL THEM TO OWN

THAT THE GALLANT BOOKSELLER
WON THRICE ALL ALONE
AND THE EDGE OF THE LAW
WAS PROVED BLUNT ON A HONE,
OH THE THREE HONEST JURIES,
HUZZAH!HUZZAH! HUZZAH!

HOW MAJESTIC IS LAW,
HOW IT SWELLS AND LOOKS BIG.
HOW TREMENDOUS ITS BROW
AND HOW AWFUL ITS WIG.
BUT THE THREE HONEST JURIES
DID NOT GIVE A FIG
FOR THE FROWN OF THE JUDGE
IN HIS AWFUL BIG WIG.
OH THE THREE HONEST JURIES,
HUZZAH! HUZZAH! HUZZAH!

THIS
IS
NOT
THE
END

**Visit samuelfrench.co.uk
and discover the best
theatre bookshop
on the internet.**

A vast range of plays
Acting and theatre books
Gifts

samuelfrench.co.uk

samuelfrenchltd

samuel french uk

Lightning Source UK Ltd.
Milton Keynes UK
UKHW02f1809140918
328921UK00005B/351/P

9 780573 115950